THE MANY LOVES OF Sarah Brennan

VIKKI ALEXANDER

Copyright © 2022 Vikki Alexander. All rights reserved

No part of this book may be reproduced or stored in a retrieval system, or transmitted in any form or by any means, electronic, mechanical, photocopying, recording, or otherwise, without express written permission of the author.

The characters and events portrayed in this book are fictitious. Any similarity to real persons, living or dead, is coincidental and not intended by the author.

All brand names or product names used in this publication are trade names, service marks, trademarks, and registered trademarks of their respective owners. The publisher and the book are not associated with any product or vendor mentioned. None of the companies referenced within the book have endorsed the book. All product, business, or brand names remain intellectual property of their registered owners.

eBook ISBN: 978-1-990724-26-8
Paperback ISBN: 978-1-990724-25-1

Cover design by MIBLart
Editing and Proofreading by Burden of Proofreading Publishing

Contents

Dedication		VI
1.	Chapter 1	1
2.	Chapter 2	5
3.	Chapter 3	12
4.	Chapter 4	17
5.	Chapter 5	27
6.	Chapter 6	36
7.	Chapter 7	40
8.	Chapter 8	49
9.	Chapter 9	53
10.	Chapter 10	59
11.	Chapter 11	64
12.	Chapter 12	70
13.	Chapter 13	74
14.	Chapter 14	76
15.	Chapter 15	79

16.	Chapter 16	83
17.	Chapter 17	86
18.	Chapter 18	90
19.	Chapter 19	95
20.	Chapter 20	99
21.	Chapter 21	104
22.	Chapter 22	109
23.	Chapter 23	112
24.	Chapter 24	117
25.	Chapter 25	120
26.	Chapter 26	127
27.	Chapter 27	133
28.	Chapter 28	142
29.	Chapter 29	147
30.	Chapter 30	154
31.	Chapter 31	158
32.	Chapter 32	161
33.	Chapter 33	165
34.	Chapter 34	169
35.	Chapter 35	179
36.	Chapter 36	184
37.	Chapter 37	189
38.	Chapter 38	192

39.	Chapter 39	198
40.	Chapter 40	203
41.	Chapter 41	206
42.	Chapter 42	210
43.	Chapter 43	215
44.	Chapter 44	220
45.	Chapter 45	224
	Acknowledgments	230
	Also By	231

In loving memory of my brother Doug
1965–2016

There are places I'll remember
All my life, though some have changed
Some forever, not for better
Some have gone and some remain
All these places have their moments
With lovers and friends, I still can recall
Some are dead and some are living
In my life, I've loved them all
The Beatles

Chapter 1

"Daddy, why do you have to go?" I fell to the floor, weeping in despair.

He knelt and lifted my chin, sweeping my hair to the side. His ice-blue eyes were peering into mine. "Sweetie, I don't have a choice. Remember, you are my sunshine, my only sunshine."

"If you stay, I'll make everything good again." I clenched my hands, begging while still on my knees. "Cross my heart."

"You're going to be fine, my princess." He kissed the top of my head, picked up his old brown leather suitcase with the fancy silver buckle, and walked out the door, leaving only a waft of the Old Spice cologne he always wore.

I remember crawling over to the door and leaning against it, wondering what I had done wrong and why he wouldn't let me go with him. My heart shattered into a thousand pieces that day.

Once the tears subsided, I walked into the kitchen, where my mom sat at the table. Her long legs were crossed, and a Virginia Slims cigarette dangled from her fingers. Her eyes were pools of sadness, and her face streaked black from wet mascara.

"Hey there, Curly Sue," she said with a sniff. She always called me that because my hair was a mass of spiral curls. The kind women pay top dollar for; at least, that's what she told me.

"Mommy, are you okay?"

Her beautiful face was sunken in pain.

"Sure am, love. Is he gone?" she asked, swiping at the wetness of her tears with a paper towel.

"Yes. When will he come back?" I crossed my fingers behind my back, hoping she would say 'soon.'

She huffed, "He's not. Do me a favor and check on your sister. She's been awfully quiet."

Before leaving, she exhaled a stream of smoke through her red-lipsticked mouth. I watched as it danced in the air, curling up around the exhaust fan over our olive-green stove.

My sister Julie and I shared a small bubble gum pink room decorated with large white daisy decals. Even though she was three, she was still in a crib, but should have been in a big girl's bed. Mom treated her like an infant, which was annoying. My heart filled with love when I walked in and looked at her through the bars. She had at least three chins and a perpetual grin. I hated to admit it, but she was adorable.

I caught myself smiling back at her, then I realized she wasn't sad. Not like me. I played back the last few years, or what I could remember, and put together that the fighting got bad when Mom's belly was big. The bigger it got, the worse the yelling. As the yelling grew louder, the hands would fly. When the hands flew, Mom would end up on the floor. I wanted them to stop, but they didn't, so Dad had to leave. Fury built in my chest. I was sure it had something to do with Julie, because Dad would never leave me. Never.

Squeezing my hand between the white slated bars, I plucked her pink pacifier out of her mouth and threw it across the room. "It's all your fault, you little shit!" I remembered Mom calling Dad that once, which made him very mad, so I knew it was bad. Then Julie screeched the way she always did when she got upset. I glared at her with my arms folded across my chest. Her smile turned to a grimace as she began to wail. "Serves you right," I whispered.

"What the hell is going on in here?" Mom roared as she stormed in.

At once, I dropped to my knees, pretending to search the floor. "She threw her pacifier. I was searching for it, but I can't find it." Okay, so I lied, but it was that, or I would have gotten in trouble.

Mom picked Julie up and rubbed her back until she calmed down. "There, there, my cheeky cherub. Sweetie, you only hurt yourself when you throw away what you want," Mom said while wiping away another round of tears, both hers and Julie's. "I want you both to listen up." She looked at me and back to Julie, still jostling her on her hip. "We are all we have," Mom stated with the utmost authority. "We must always stick together, no matter what. Sarah, do you understand?"

My head bobbed in silent response.

From that day forward, it was only me, Mom, and Julie. "The Girls," as my grandpa dubbed us. Being 'The Girls' had its perks. Mom would take me into her room at night and paint my toenails fire engine red. After she painted my tiny nails, we lay in her bed watching grown-up movies where people kissed with their eyes closed. Mom drank her wine in a goblet the size of the globe on my desk, and I had apple juice in one of the glasses that once held grape jelly.

"Now remember, Sarah, these are movies. They are not real life." I recall her saying in the same voice my teachers used in school.

"What do you mean?"

"I mean, 'happily ever after' is a fairytale that movie executives created to make us long for the impossible. They've used it to cripple women, but they don't fool me."

I was more confused than ever.

She pointed her long finger at the man in the dark suit. "You see that man? I want you to notice how he looks at the woman sitting on the couch. He's looking at her with lust. Do you understand what lust is?"

"No, Mommy."

"Lust is like a magnet that pulls us toward something or someone. In this case, a man and a woman. The woman in the movie doesn't realize that she can convince him to do whatever she wants when he has that look."

Snuggling up closer to her, I was breathing the same air. I could smell the sweet wine and nicotine on her breath. "Is that what happened with you and Daddy?"

"Your father and I once looked like the couple in that movie, but I didn't know the secrets back then. There are secrets to being a woman, and I will teach them to you." She gave the tip of my nose a little tap. "Curly, this is a crucial lesson. You must not, under any circumstance, allow a man to control you. Do you understand me?"

"Got it, Mom." I put my little hand on her face, feeling her cheek swell with her smile. I missed my dad so much that it hurt my stomach, but I adored my mom. After he left, Mom and I became one. The Brennan Girls.

Chapter 2

When Dad left, so did the money. I could still hear the crashing of pots and pans as they hit the wall in a fit of anger. The clanging noise was only outdone by Mom screaming, "God damn it, that bastard didn't send the money again!" Julie and I would hide in the corner, holding each other until her rant ran its course.

Sometimes she didn't have enough money to pay the electric bill, and the apartment would be dark for days. Mom insisted it was Dad's fault because he didn't send the 'goddamn money.' This went on for about two years, but everything changed when my grandparents gave us the most incredible present ever.

That day stayed etched in my memory. It was a Friday, and the sky was the same shade of blue I dyed my Easter eggs. I skipped to the car, full of excitement, because it was the weekend I got to be with Dad. I hopped into the backseat with Julie. "Hey, Squirt, how was baby school?" I patted her on the head the way I had watched my father do so many times before.

"Sarah, don't do that; it's not nice," Mom reprimanded me.

"Sorry, Mom. How was kindergarten, Julie?"

"It was so much fun. I made this for you." She handed over a paper card that had 'To the best big sister ever' scrawled in green crayon and what could pass for flowers in the corner. Maybe she wasn't so bad.

"Mom, where are we going? This isn't the way home," I said frantically once I realized we were not on our way back to our apartment building.

"It's a surprise." Mom grinned at me in the rearview mirror.

We pulled up to a one-story brick ranch house that had a welcoming white door with glass cutouts in the shape of half circles. Outside stood a sign with a red SOLD placard on it. Grandma stood on the steps wearing her mink stole and trademark pearls. Grandpa was by her side in a tweed jacket and a brown felt hat with a red feather protruding from the band. They both waved from the front steps as we pulled into the driveway.

I unbuckled my seatbelt as quickly as possible and ran over to them through the overgrown grass. "Are you guys moving here?" I panted excitedly.

They both smiled and shook their heads.

"No," Grandma said curtly, with a smirk.

I scowled at Grandpa. "What's going on?" I placed my hands on my hip and began tapping my foot, appearing very serious.

He didn't answer; his face kept his unrevealed secret.

Mom came behind me and dangled a silver key in front of my eyes. "Welcome home, Curly Sue. Do you like our new house?" She giggled as she spoke.

"No way," I shrieked.

"Way." She mimicked my stance.

Looking around, I was dumbfounded. We were actually going to have a house. No more having to be quiet because of the cranky old neighbors down the hall. Julie and I could run around and play tag. We could have a sprinkler to jump through during the summer. Not only that, but there was a giant tree right in front with the biggest leaves I had ever seen. "Mom, can we get a tire swing for the tree?" I begged, being reminded of my favorite Christmas movie, *Miracle on 34th Street*. That little girl got a swing, and I wanted one too.

"We'll see. Now run off with your sister and explore the backyard while I grab some boxes from the car."

As Julie and I rounded the corner, I peeked back. Mom was clinging to Grandpa with her head on his shoulder, and he was stroking her hair. It was the first time I had witnessed any tenderness pass between them.

Our lives were becoming more normal, like other kids, but with only one parent living at home. Now that we had a house, mom needed a job, so she got one. Her options were limited since she never graduated from college or went to secretarial school. Mom went back to doing what she did best. Singing and entertaining the masses at a fancy hotel by the river.

Nightclub life may sound glamorous to some, but not when you are the nightclub singer's daughter. Between rehearsals and her jobs, she was seldom home. Our Grandparents hired Betty, a lovely Irish woman who spoke in a broken cadence, to take care of us. At first, she came across as very strict, but her softer side came out over time. She always smelled like my favorite cookie, snickerdoodles. It was as if she rolled in cinnamon and spice before coming over.

"Hey there, little miss," she said one night while tucking me in. "Why so glum, chum?" she questioned, brushing my hair away from my eyes.

"I miss my mom. It's bad enough that Dad isn't here, but now she's not here too!" Tears rolled down the side of my face onto the white pillowcase.

"Hush now, sweet girl. Your mom works hard to give you all the wonderful things you deserve. You need to be patient."

"It's so hard, Betty. It's like I'm an orphan!" My body shook as I sobbed even harder.

"What do you know about being an orphan? I can tell you stories about being an orphan in my country."

"No, not the potato famine again." I cringed.

"Oh yes, young lady. Those were hard times, and the children were real orphans. You're just being silly. You have a mom and dad who both love you. I know they both seem terribly busy right now, but I promise everything will sort itself out if you give it time. That's how life works. Time and patience, patience and time." She kissed me on the forehead and smoothed out my covers. "How about tomorrow we go down to Woolworth's and get some ice cream sundaes? Would you like that?"

Despite my tears, I nodded my head emphatically.

"Very well," she whispered as she crossed the room to tuck in Julie, who was fast asleep in her bed.

After Betty left, I curled up in a ball, hugging my knees and my stuffed giraffe as close to my chest as possible, wishing that someone understood why I was so sad. I pulled the pillow over my head to muffle my sobs; after all, big girls don't cry.

Mom was always running around with weird men, and Dad kept getting married. About a year after Dad moved out of the apartment, he married wife number two. Her name was Denise. She was a hairdresser who wore a giant blonde beehive on her head. She stank of bleach and gawked at us with disdain. That wife lasted about a year, and then he married Claudette. She was fake nice. When dad was around, she was all smiles and ice cream, but when he wasn't, she was mean. Once, she locked Jul and me in the backyard and wouldn't let us in. We sat in the grass for three hours, trying to keep ourselves entertained with a game of 'What if,' waiting for Dad to come home. The best one was when Julie asked, "What if... Mom and Dad still loved each other, and we could be a family again?" How I wished we could make that 'What if' a reality, but instead, we were covered in itchy mosquito bites from head to toe, locked outside like pound puppies.

Wife three wouldn't let him see us every other weekend, which was how it was supposed to happen. He said she was sad because she couldn't have her own babies. Maybe that's true, but that was no reason to be mean to us. She must have gotten sick of us or the nasty phone calls from Mom because Claudette packed up her bags and left, which was fine with me. All I wanted was to spend time with my mom and dad.

Spending the holidays or weekends with my father was always magical. I would anxiously sit by the window in an old needlepoint wing chair, awaiting the roar of his Porsche. It would declare his arrival like a trumpet announcing a king. His car was jet black, like my hair—I was sure that's why he picked it—and it was fast. The people on the sidewalks were a blur when we rocketed past them. Sometimes, he would let me sit on his lap and steer. We didn't tell mom. She would have had a hissy fit. I loved when it was only the two of us. Dad would tell me exciting stories of when he was in the Air Force and all the faraway places he traveled. His deep voice painted verbal pictures of white sand beaches and the bluest water of the Mediterranean, where you could see your feet. When he spoke of jungles and plucking wounded men from combat in Vietnam, it was nothing short of heroic. My father was my king, and I was his princess.

Sadly, the holiday, birthday, or weekend would end, and he would have to leave me. I desperately wanted to go with him, but he insisted it was better for little girls to live with their mothers. As he would leave, he would give me a bear hug, lifting me off the ground. "Who's my sunshine?" he'd ask.

That was our thing. He asked the question, and I would reply, "I am!"

On the way out, he would tussle Julie's hair and say, "Goodbye, little one." It didn't occur to me until much later that he didn't hug or kiss her. When he spoke to her, it was almost as if he was looking through her.

After several months, Mom started making enough money that we no longer needed to be on food stamps. Mom became popular with the other employees and regular hotel guests. She would throw glamorous parties where she would sing better than anyone you would hear on the radio. I would peek out my door and watch as all eyes were on her.

"Jackie, sing something special, just for me," called a dark bearded man standing in the corner holding a glass of amber liquid.

"Anything for you, stud," she purred back and winked.

Mom closed her eyes and began to sway. The first line of *When A Man Loves A Woman* flowed from her lips with incredible power but also with a gentleness that left both her friends and me in a hypnotic-like trance.

When the song was over, she came to speak to me. "Alright, Curly Sue, time for the door to stay closed. This is an adults-only party. You and Julie can play for a little while longer and then put yourselves to bed. Okay?"

"Okay, Mom." I was utterly disappointed.

Over time, I studied my mom intently, learning to mimic her moves. Her motions were more of a slither than how most women moved. Touching my developing body, I tried to work it with intent. I deliberately put strands of hair behind my ear with my head slightly cocked. I smiled a crooked smile. It was not the cheesy one you made for a camera. It was the kind that said you had a secret. I practiced in the mirror for hours until I had it down pat.

I was determined to have people look at me the way they looked at Mom.

Chapter 3

NO ONE IN OUR town ever considered me one of them. I was the unwelcome divorcee's daughter. Mom always said the other women were jealous. They didn't have our freedom, and certainly, they didn't have our beauty. The only thing they had was money, and well, that comes and goes. One of Mom's favorite expressions was 'beauty may only be skin deep, but ugly is to the bone.'

A new girl, Debbie, came to our school in seventh grade. Mrs. Blackwell, our teacher, made her stand in front of the class and tell us all about herself. She got up before twenty-five strangers, explaining how her father got a new job in Edison, which was why they moved to Westfield. They were from Iowa, where there was a lot of corn and not much else. Her face turned red, almost the same shade as her hair. She dug her hands so deeply into the pockets of her purple Jordache jeans, I glimpsed a hint of her pink panties.

"Hey, hold up a minute," I called out to Debbie as she walked out of class.

Scanning around in all directions, she mouthed, "Me?"

"Yes, you. Welcome to hell." I smirked. "Only kidding. It's not so bad. Do you know anyone yet?"

"No, not a soul. Did I look like a total dipshit up there?" She was understandably self-conscious.

"Not at all. You looked a little uncomfortable, but who wouldn't be when you're on display like that? I probably would have passed out." I extended my hand. "I'm Sarah Brennan. It's nice to meet you."

"Nice to meet you too." She pumped my hand several times. "You already know my name, right?" she asked with a hint of hesitation.

"Yeah, of course. Would you like to walk around town after school? We can share a Tab or something."

Relief washed over her as a smile appeared. "That would be really cool. Thanks so much."

After school, we met by the flagpole and headed over to Broad Street.

"So, is this your first time in Jersey?"

"Yes, I've never been anywhere except Iowa. Everything and everyone is so different from the Midwest. After school, the only things to do were smoke weed or work on a farm."

"Which did you choose?" I asked, hoping for a specific answer.

"Let's put it this way; I didn't work on a farm."

We cracked up.

As luck would have it, Debbie moved only two blocks away from our house on Cottage, which was amazing to have a built-in friend.

One night, we snuck off to the playground around the corner. We drifted back and forth on the creaky metal swings as we passed a bottle of vodka I stole from my mom.

"I want to show you something." Debbie slid an old photo with bent corners out of her rear pocket. "This is my mom." Her voice caught as she passed it my way.

"Wow, you look like twins, right down to the freckle on the side of your nose," I said in disbelief, looking from the photo to Debbie and back again.

"I know. That's why my dad can't stand to look at me." The tears came. She held out her hand to take the photo back and pressed it to her heart. "I miss her so much. Nothing has been the same since she died."

I always thought it was hard being the kid with the mom everyone gossiped about, but at least I knew my dad loved me. I didn't know what to say, so I didn't say anything at all.

"Sarah, thank you so much for being my friend. I've been so alone. I'm going to tell you a secret, but you have to promise not to say a word to anyone," she said, staring at the ground.

I made an 'x' in front of my body. "Cross my heart, hope to die."

"I have been thinking about killing myself."

An unintentional gasp escaped, which I tried to silence by covering my mouth.

"I'm sorry. I shouldn't have told you." She stopped, obviously regretting telling me her secret.

"No, don't be sorry. You can tell me anything. I totally get it." I took her hand. "We are in this together." I knew what it was like to feel isolated and different from everyone else. If her dad wasn't going to look after her, I would. We stayed that way until our eyes grew heavy from the liquor, and the owls began their calls into the dark night. That was the start of our relationship. At last, I had a best friend to tell my secrets. Neither of us would be lonely anymore.

During the summer between middle school and high school, I got my period, and everything changed. Overnight I developed sizable round breasts and slender womanly hips. Mom and I went to the local department store to purchase a few new items to go with the metamorphosis. She bought me two push-up bras, one white and one black. We also got a couple of cotton T-shirts with a deep v, exposing my new cleavage, and skin tight Sassoon jeans that hugged my bottom.

I remember strolling into the cafeteria on the first day of freshman year, scanning the room for Debbie. My underarms were growing damper by the second. I only hoped no one would see me pitting out. I kept my arms folded down like a chicken wing while continuing to scan the room.

"Hey, check out Sarah," a voice called.

"Holy shit, what happened to you?" yelled another while making an hourglass figure with his hands.

Biting my lower lip, I held my books a little tighter and sat down at the round table near the window. I knew I was being watched. I tucked a loose strand of long curly black hair behind my ear, as I had practiced years before, and glanced at the boys out of the corner of my eye. They were hooked, and so was I. Hooked on the power my new body gave me and the thrill of the attention. I glided through high school with various boys begging for my attention.

The boys would wait for me at my locker or outside my class. Some I dated for weeks, others for months, but nothing that meant anything—at least not for me. They were my subjects. I listened and learned from their wants and desires, knowing the information would serve me well in the future.

Debbie and I ruled the school. Boys loved us, girls wanted to be us, and who could blame them? We were invited to all the most fabulous parties and got out of trouble by batting our eyelashes at the adult in charge. We were untouchable.

By my senior year, I was suffocating. High School was useless, and the boys', children. Nothing changed between Mom and Dad, and Julie was such a child.

Graduation couldn't come soon enough. I was desperate to escape the small-town mentality and experience the real world.

In the meantime, every day at three o'clock, I would hustle from school to my job at the local convenience store. Checking my watch, I saw I was five minutes late. "Damn it." I ran the last block, knowing my shift leader would fire me if I was late one more day.

As I approached the glass door, the pulsating sound of AC/DC made me turn around. That's when I met him—the one who took my breath away.

He leaned against his pimped-out cherry red mustang, flashing a smoldering smile that sent a ripple throughout my body. "Hey, I'm lost. Can you tell me where the closest gas station is? I'm running on fumes." The twinkle in his eye was electrifying. They were a magnificent shade of cerulean blue that made my knees tremble. His chiseled chin was covered in dark stubble and had matching dimples on his dreamy, symmetrical face.

"You're not from around here, huh?" I tried to sound calm, but my stammer gave me away.

"My mom and I moved here last week. I'm all kinds of turned around. Maybe you could give me a tour sometime?" he said, checking me out from head to toe.

YES! YES! YES! I screamed in my head but casually replied, "Sure, do you want my number?" Head tilt, hair strand, crooked smile.

Chapter 4

ONCE I MET JIMMY, nothing else mattered. Debbie and I stopped hanging out, and my grades plummeted, but I didn't care. I had always had an emptiness deep inside that I refused to acknowledge, but with Jimmy, that place was bursting with his love.

We spent most of our time in his basement, laying on his brown futon while having philosophical discussions and smoking weed. He was sexier than James Dean in *Rebel Without a Cause*. How had Mom not told me that was possible? Did she not know, or was she intentionally keeping it a secret? Either way, she was wrong. Love is both real and magical.

One sunny afternoon, we headed to the Alpine lookout, where we could view the sailboats gliding down the Hudson River. The breeze blew my hair in front of my eyes, blinding me for a moment as we were climbing onto a rock that jutted out high above the river. My ankle twisted on the rubble as I stepped down, throwing me off-kilter. A guttural cry escaped me as I headed toward the edge. At that exact moment, Jimmy wrapped both arms around my waist, bringing me back to safety.

"Sarah, you have to be more careful. Nothing can ever happen to you." Terror overtook his handsome face, and his breath was shallow. "Promise me. Promise me you'll be more careful."

"Promise. I'm so sorry. I don't know how that happened." My body was shaking uncontrollably.

"I know I don't say it a lot, but I need you to know that I love you and can't imagine a day without you."

I took his face in my hands and kissed him hard. Harder than I had ever kissed anyone. An emotional explosion rocked my world.

Graduation day was at last upon me. I donned my cap and gown, glancing at myself with approval. After the ceremony, I would be a free woman. I would be Jimmy's woman. My life was on the precipice of happening, and the anticipation was overwhelming.

I sat amongst a sea of black gowns waiting for my name to be called. When it was my turn, I strolled up to the stage with a purpose. Once there, I scanned the crowd for the only person who mattered. He was sitting between Jackie and Joe, otherwise known as Mom and Dad. Of course, Julie was there too, but *he* was the one I longed to see.

The roar of the crowd erupted once we switched our tassels over. We were free. We graduated.

"Mom! Mom!" I called out into the crowd.

When I got their attention, Mom yelled above the din. "Congratulations, Curly Sue! I'm so proud of you."

"Congratulations, Sarah! You look so beautiful," Julie chimed in as I closed the gap between my family and myself.

"Thanks, Squirt!" I ruffled her hair as I sidled up next to her.

"There's my princess! I'm so proud of you. Come back to your mom's house. I have something to show you." Dad was as giddy as a schoolgirl.

Before Dad could tell me the rest, Jimmy grabbed me. "You are a rockstar," he said, picking me up off my feet.

"Babe, I'm gonna run. I have a zillion things to do before our trip. Meet me later?"

"Of course." I kissed him discreetly, knowing everyone was watching.

I jumped in the passenger's seat of Dad's Porsche as Julie and Mom followed in our banged-up old brown Buick.

As we turned the corner onto our street, I spied a beige LeBaron Convertible sitting in the driveway with a giant white bow. "Oh my god, Dad! No way!" I shrieked.

"Yes, way!" He gave me a side glance. "But you have to promise to be careful." He took my hand and squeezed it three times.

When the car rolled to a stop, I bolted out and ran over to inspect my new wheels. Mom and Julie showed up a few seconds later.

"Dad, can I take it to show Jimmy?"

"Sure, honey. Please be back in an hour. We're having a family dinner, and you're the guest of honor."

I jumped up and snatched the keys from his finger. "I love you so much, Daddy," I yelled as I hopped into the car and turned on the ignition. Before the engine roared to life, I unlocked the roof anchors and slid down the brown rag top. "Love you too, Mom," I called as an afterthought while backing out of the driveway.

Jimmy lived in Plainfield, a couple of towns over. We practically lived in his basement over the last three months. That is where we planned our future. We had highlighted the maps to show our route to California, and our backpacks were ready to go. One more night, and we were out of there.

I pulled up to his house and ogled from afar as he mowed his lawn without a shirt. God, the sight of him made me melt. The six-pack that ran along his abdomen was my trail to ecstasy. Looking at him never got old.

When Jimmy finally caught me spying, he called out, "Hey babe, bitching ride!" as he strolled over my way.

"Can you believe it? Pop gave it to me. We can take it out west."

He took both of my hands in his. "Whatever you want. Are we still good to celebrate tonight?"

"Of course. First, I have to have dinner with the parental units." I rolled my eyes. "I'll meet you back here at ten o'clock?"

"Sure thing, babe." He grabbed me by the waist and kissed me intensely.

Dinner was a struggle. Being with Mom, Dad, and Julie was exhausting. I couldn't tell if my parents loved or despised each other. Sometimes, when they thought no one was looking, their eyes met, and they'd do some kind of bizarre flirting, which was weird since they constantly fought about money. Their relationship was uber confusing.

After dinner, I couldn't drive to Jimmy's fast enough. As soon as I arrived, I jumped in his car, and with a kiss, we were off to our favorite joint to celebrate. I ripped out my ponytail and flung my head out the window, enjoying the first night of our forever together.

There was an audible 'tick tick tick' of the car's directional signal as he pulled off the Garden State Parkway.

"Jimmy, where are we going?" I glanced around tentatively, being somewhat reminded of a horror movie I had recently seen.

"What's the matter? Are you scared?" he mocked.

I stuck my tongue out at him in response.

The road twisted and turned between giant trees, which opened up to a massive lake with the full moon reflecting off the water. Before I had a chance to ask any questions, he jumped out of the car and ran to my side to open the door.

"After you, my lady." He bowed in the most gentlemanly fashion.

"Jimmy, where are we?" I leered at him suspiciously, unsure of what was going on.

"I come here when I need to think or talk with dad to get some fatherly advice. I know he can't answer, but I feel closer to him when I'm here."

The sky glittered with a million stars. The big dipper and Orion's belt twinkled brightly, allowing me to see them for the first time in my life. "This is incredible."

When I turned toward him, he was down on the ground with one knee sinking into the dark sand. A sparkle glimmered from the box he was holding.

"Sarah Brennan, love of my life. Will you marry me?"

Without hesitation, I cried, "Yes!"

Jimmy popped up and twirled me around and around until the world was a series of streaks of light. Once everything returned right side up, reality spoiled the moment. "There is no way my folks will go for this."

He stared so deeply into my eyes, I swear he was able to see my soul. "Don't worry, I already thought of that. Wear my ring tonight, and when we get home, you give it back. Once we hit Cali, you, me, and a Justice of the Peace have a date. They won't be able to stop us."

"Perfect. Exactly like you." I brought him in close. Having his muscular body against me made me feel like nothing bad could ever happen.

We eventually made our way to our destination, The Crow's House, a small, dimly lit bar that played fantastic rock. The Grateful Dead and The Who pulsated through the speaker's night and day, and a trace odor of urinal cakes could be smelled lingering below the surface.

"Listen up," Jimmy bellowed across the bar. "Today, my baby graduated from high school." Everyone lifted their glasses. "Hold on, hold on." He held up his hand to quiet everyone down. "That's not all. This magnificent creature has agreed to be my wife." The crowd erupted in hoots and hollers.

"To Sarah," everyone cheered in unison.

"To Jimmy and Sarah," toasted Benji, the bartender.

We sang *Sweet Home Alabama* into our fists while standing on the old wood bar. The other patrons waved their lighters in approval. Between songs, we licked salt off each other's necks and threw back a shot of tequila, followed by a bite of tart lemon that made our mouths pucker. It was the best night of my life.

The clock read two in the morning, and Benji was ready to close. Jimmy's friends high-fived him on our way out, and I received many warm hugs. They called out well wishes as we strolled across the parking lot hand in hand.

We careened down the parkway at speeds topping ninety miles an hour. The windows were open, and so was the road. My hair blew in the wind like a wild mop as we screamed the lyrics of our favorite songs into the night air.

Red flashing lights broke up the darkness. In the distance, a shadowy figure was talking about something that didn't make sense: "We have four DOA, two of them juveniles."

I felt small hard pebbles scratching at the palm of my hand, and my head was aching. When I tried to lift myself up, everything swam in and out of focus. I lay back down, trying to make the world stop spinning. "What's going on? Where's Jimmy?" My voice creaked.

Another kinder voice replied, "Hush now, you're going to be okay. Let me bandage you up, and then we can talk about everything." Her hands worked quickly.

The strobe lights were making me dizzy. The police, ambulance, and fire trucks were lining the roadway. My confusion grew as I took in my surroundings. "What the fuck happened?" I muttered to no one in particular.

That's when the officer I had heard on the radio came over to speak with me.

"Is she okay to talk?" the police officer consulted with the medic. I tried to make out his face, but it was obscured by the kaleidoscope of lights.

"She's lucky. It appears she only sustained cuts and bruises. I braced her neck just in case."

The medic placed one hand on my back and the other on my arm to help me sit up. My body rebelled in pain as if I had been beaten up.

"Hi, what's your name?" The cop's voice was less than friendly.

"Sarah. Sarah Brennan. Where's Jimmy?"

"Well, Sarah. This is how it is; Jimmy didn't make it." His voice was matter of fact.

"What? What are you talking about, didn't make it?" I barked at him.

"Sarah, were you partying?" He raised a singular eyebrow. "No need to answer; we already know."

None of this made any sense. No one was on the road. We were singing. For fuck's sake, we were just singing.

"Sarah, are you still with me?" The cop snapped his fingers in front of my eyes.

The scent of burning rubber permeated my nose. Several yards away, two cars were intertwined, metal upon metal, making a strange sculpture of sorts. Half of it was red and the other half silver. Laying by the sculpture were canvas tarps. I moved as if being operated by remote control, mindlessly heading toward the unknown heap. A firm grip on my arm stopped me from moving further.

"I would not suggest going over there, hon. Give me your address; I'll send someone to get your parents." Everything around me began to swim. The cop grabbed my elbow and eased me down gradually to the curb. I didn't cry. I didn't scream. The expression paralyzed with grief was familiar to me, and in that moment, I understood what it meant.

I was both cold and numb at the same time while watching the chaos around me for what felt like hours until I spotted Julie streaking through the night. "Oh my god, Sarah; are you okay?"

"Jul, he's dead. My Jimmy's dead."

She put her arm around me and held my shivering body.

"He's dead. He's dead. He's dead," was all I could sputter out.

When we returned home, Julie and Mom helped me to the couch, and Mom brought me water.

As I reached for the glass, Julie grabbed my hand. "What's this, Sarah?" Her mouth was agape, and her brown eyes bulged out of their sockets.

I had completely forgotten that I was still wearing his ring. "We're going to get married when we get to California." I held my hand out, watching the small stone glitter in the lamplight.

Julie glanced at Mom, and mom glanced at me.

"What? What are you looking at?" I snapped.

"Sarah, you do understand what happened tonight, don't you?" Mom's voice was so soft, it sounded nothing like her.

"Of course, I fucking understand. Do you think I'm an idiot? The love of my life is dead. Now get the hell off my back." I hobbled into my bedroom on my aching legs and slammed the door so hard that the light fixtures rattled.

The ring on my finger and a few pieces of clothing were the only things I had left of the man I loved. The crying jags would appear without warning. It was as if I had lost my mind and no longer had control over my body.

The funeral was held at the old brick church in the town where he lived with his mother. The white steeple that jutted into the heavens was visible from miles away. Jimmy had brought me there once when we first started to date. He wasn't religious, but he had these sweet little idealisms that he brought with him from his youth.

On the church property was a lovely free-form pond where mallard ducks floated around in endless circles. As a little boy, his father took him to a pond like that, where he grew up in Texas. They would bring a loaf of stale bread to feed the ducks. It was one of many cherished memories he had of them together.

Paula, Jimmy's mom, and I sat in the front pew, clenching each other's hands so tightly that they turned white. Mom and Julie sat behind us in support. The warmth of my sister's hand on my shoulder helped to keep me present. The silence all around was deafening.

The creak of the church doors echoed down the long aisle; my body shuttered in response. I prayed to God for the strength to stand and watch the procession. As Paula and I rose, we braced against each other for balance. The rosewood casket glided down the aisle, flanked by his closest friends. An array of colors from the stained glass bounced off the polished wood.

Paula clenched my hand even tighter. "He was all I had left. Jimmy was the only thing that kept me sane when his father died, and now he's gone," she choked out each word.

Standing against the wall in the back of the church, I spotted Debbie lurking. Our eyes locked, and the memory of our last encounter ran through my head. She was waiting outside of the store when I left work one night. Her hair was a brighter shade of fiery red than ever; it was as if her anger saturated the color. Her neck was blotched with rage. "What the fuck, Sarah? You never answer my phone calls. You act like you don't know me in the halls. It's as if the last six years never happened. Why have you ditched me?"

The last thing I wanted to do after a long day was deal with Debbie's adolescent nonsense. "Deb, it's nothing personal. Someday, you'll understand," I assured her. "Jimmy and I are in love, and I don't have time for the little girl games anymore."

As I spoke, she bit the inside of her cheek, as she often did when she was pissed off. "Yeah, you're so fucking grown up, Sarah." She was obviously being sarcastic. "You were the one who taught me the girl code, sisters before misters. Fuck you," she shrieked and stormed off.

The day's pain returned as the Priest took to the pulpit and began the homily. I tried to find meaning in the words he spoke, but was overwhelmed by the perfume of the floral arrangements flanking both sides of the altar. They held cascades of white lilies which exuded a sickly sweet scent that permeated the air, constricting my esophagus. It's funny the things that come to the foreground when you are numb. The stream of tears flowed in a torrent of pain. Our bodies were heaving as we gasped for air.

The thought of life continuing was inconceivable.

Chapter 5

ONCE THE FUNERAL WAS over, my chest was perpetually tight, making me feel as if I was suffocating. I paced my bedroom back and forth like a caged animal, leaving a worn path in my wake. I dragged on cigarettes until the red tip reached the yellow filter, then lit another. The glass ashtray was filled to the brim with the stale remains. My brain was a jigsaw puzzle that I couldn't piece back together.

All night, the black and white portable television flickered with images of beautiful people losing the love of their lives. Starlets cried into their pillows and threw vases against the wall. I took a small measure of comfort in sharing my pain with them, even if the characters weren't real.

"Sarah, please!" Julie whined. "I need to sleep. School is starting tomorrow. It's really important that I do well this year."

"Shut up, you little twat!" As soon as the words came out of my mouth, I regretted them. "Sorry, Jul. I'm such a mess. I didn't mean it. Do you want to get in bed with me? We can cuddle."

Julie climbed in, snuggling in close. As she lay next to me, I grasped that she was no longer a little girl;

sometime over the last few months, she had become a young woman when I wasn't looking. I stared down at her heart-shaped face, wanting to take back all the mean things I often said to her. I wrapped my arm around her as she drifted off.

Mom took me to see Marty, our family doctor. She thought that since I wasn't sleeping or eating, he might be able to help. After a thorough examination and a million questions, we sat down at his oversized, self-important desk to have a "discussion."

"Jackie, she's depressed," Marty addressed my mother.

"I'm sitting right here." I waved my arms, showing I wasn't invisible. "You can talk to me. I am legally an adult."

"Sorry, you're right, Sarah. You give every indication of being depressed, and with good reason." His voice was kind and reassuring. "I'm going to give you a prescription. It will help level you out a bit, but remember, this is a drug and should not be abused or misused. We will check back in six months to see how you're doing. Does that work?"

I nodded in the affirmative.

The little white pill did its job. At long last, I was able to sleep. It was the kind of sleep that didn't give you dreams. As I lay on my bed, staring at the ceiling, I wondered if my new 'sleep' was what Jimmy was feeling, but that was stupid because dead people don't feel. At least, I didn't think they did.

I doubled down on the pills, but the sinking sensation didn't abate. I went to the Crow's House to see if any of our old friends could help. Since that fateful night, I hadn't been back. Sympathetic faces rushed to greet me on the other side of the heavy swinging door. The sting of my loss engulfed me again at the outpouring of love.

After an hour of small talk and a couple of beers, I got what I came for. The small bag of white powder left a lump in my rear pocket. Once I got home, I sank into oblivion. The combination of drugs usually did the trick. Sometimes adding a shot of vodka sped up the process. The weeks sailed by in a sleepy numbness. It was kind of like the Pink Floyd lyrics, *comfortably numb*.

Sometime later, I didn't know how long; fragments of noise came from somewhere outside my darkened hideaway. I couldn't drag myself out of the deep, hazy abyss. I wanted to remain engulfed in the serene waters.

"Sarah, wake up." The voice sounded far away and scared. "Sarah, wake up." It had grown louder. My body was being shaken violently by the outside force. "Sarah, what the hell is going on?" My father was standing over me when I opened my eyes, his complexion ruddy with fear.

"Nothing, Dad, I'm fine. I need to sleep, that's all," I slurred and rolled back over.

"Bullshit, you are not fine." He grabbed me by my limp arms, raising me to a sitting position.

My head flopped to one side.

"Julie, pack a bag for your sister," he barked. "Jesus Christ, Sarah. What the hell have you done?"

"Where are you taking her?" Julie wanted to know from somewhere in the distance.

"Shut up and do as you're told," he snapped.

The next thing I knew, Dad placed me in the bucket seat of his car. "Damn it, Jackie, you should have called me sooner." Dad was yelling at mom as I rested my head on the window.

"If you weren't so busy with your new wife, maybe you would have noticed what's happening. I can only do so much alone," she hissed back.

"Forget it. I'll take it from here," he snarled. As we pulled out of the driveway, my little sister was staring out our bedroom window. I think she was crying.

We drove past horse farms and cow pastures for what seemed like forever. It was a blur of greens and browns. After several hours, we turned down a dirt road leading to an old white manor with fluted columns in front. Chipped black paint outlined the words Rochester Psychiatric and Rehabilitation Clinic.

"Ah, fuck," I mumbled.

The first days were the hardest. While my body expelled the remnants of the drugs in my system, I shivered as if lying naked in the snow. I would have given anything to get high. They attached a yellow bag to my arm that fed me droplets of nutrients.

The subsequent week, I started both group and individual therapy. They held group sessions in a cavernous room where twenty metal chairs were set up in a circle. I chose the one closest to the door.

A stout, red-headed woman approached before I had the chance to sit. She wore a paper name tag that read Becca. "Since you're new to the group, it's the protocol for you to introduce yourself first. Do you know what to say?"

I had watched enough after-school specials to know the drill. "Do I really have to say it? It's so cliché," I huffed.

"Yes. It's required of all our group patients," she stated sternly. "When you see me point, that's your sign to begin."

I knew I wouldn't be able to talk my way out of it. Becca may have had a name that sounded sweet and fun, like she should be frolicking in a field, but she was neither of those. She had the ability to make my life a living hell, and I had no doubt she would secretly enjoy it. *Tick a lock*, I reminded myself.

Once everyone had taken their seat, Becca gave the signal.

"Hi, my name is Sarah, and I'm a drug addict." It was such bullshit that I had to say that phrase because it wasn't true. I was trying to shut out the pain of losing Jimmy. Anyone with half a brain should be able to see that.

"Hi Sarah," rang the voices encircling me.

A disheveled boy sat directly across from me wearing a Rolling Stones T-shirt, jeans with a rip in the knee, and scuffed-up Timberlands. He appeared to be studying his cuticles while rapidly bouncing his leg up and down.

"Robbie, could you please pay attention?" chided Becca.

He begrudgingly looked up, but his leg never stopped moving.

The tales of woe that gushed from all the other teens were totally lame. It was all: my mom doesn't understand me, my dad is a prick, blah, blah. That is, until it came to Robbie.

"Robbie, why don't you go now? It's been a couple of weeks since you've said anything," Becca urged in a way that was more of a directive than a request.

Before speaking, he inhaled deeply as if he was about to go underwater and began to play with the loose threads by the knee of his jeans. "Hi, my name is Robbie, and I'm a drug addict."

In unison, the room echoed, "Hi Robbie."

"I can't believe you're making me do this. This is so stupid. My story hasn't changed." His eyes were pleading with Becca to let him off the hook, to which she shot him a stare that spoke louder than words.

"Fine." He grimaced. "Hi, my name is Robbie, and I'm a drug addict," he repeated. Then he rattled off his story as if it was lines of a play. When he was done, we were all dismissed. He vanished out the double doors into the fresh air, and I was compelled to follow him.

I trailed behind, hoping he wouldn't see me.

He abruptly turned around, catching me off guard. "Why are you following me?" His face was soft, which led me to believe he was more curious than annoyed.

The heat in my cheeks grew to an uncomfortable level. "Sorry. I'm not a creeper or anything. All the kids in here act like self-indulgent brats with too much time on their hands." My eyes pleaded with him to understand my plight.

He half giggled with a headshake. "So, Miss Judgy, what does that make me?"

"Authentic. You have a real story. An honest to God reason for why you got hooked."

"Yeah, well, wish I didn't," he huffed, kicking at the loose dirt on the ground.

"Me too," I said sadly, visualizing Jimmy's casket on the church altar. "Would you mind if we hung out a bit? I don't know anyone, and I could use someone to talk to who's not a shrink or a narcissistic teen."

Later that afternoon, I had my first one-on-one session with my therapist, Megan, a bright and bubbly personality with coke-bottle glasses, caked-on blue eye shadow, and bright pink lipstick. She held a yellow-lined notepad and a ballpoint pen. I sat in the chair across from her with my appendages twisted like a pretzel, listening to her rattle-off questions that really had no bearing on my current situation.

"Sarah, this will go much smoother if you participate," Megan advised.

I read the situation and delved into my bag of tricks, the same ones I used in high school. Over the ensuing months, I wept when it was expected, got angry, and went through all the stages of grief until I reached the last one, acceptance, or so it appeared. It took three months, two weeks, and four days. All the while, my flirtation with Robbie kept me distracted from the constant ache in my heart.

"Sarah, do you think you're ready to go home?" Megan asked one day, seemingly out of the blue. What an idiotic question. Of course, I was ready. I was ready when Dad dropped me off, but I knew the words that would set me free.

"Megan, losing Jimmy was the hardest thing I have ever experienced, but I understand self-medication is not the answer. It only makes things worse." I conceded like a good little brainwashed robot. "There are people who love me and will support me. I promise to reach out to them instead of pills or alcohol." I smiled and shook my head, showing her the depth of my understanding. "Megan, thank you for giving me back my life," I added to seal the deal while cringing inside.

"I'm so glad to hear that. The other therapists and I have agreed we no longer think you pose a danger to yourself or anyone else. I called home, and someone will be here to pick you up in the morning." She seemed absurdly proud of herself, as if she had achieved some kind of miracle.

After leaving Megan's office, I ran outside to tell Robbie the good news. I found him lying on 'our bench', reading a beat-up old detective novel with yellowed pages. The information flew out so fast that I was out of breath once delivered.

He sat up, unfurled his body, and began the frenetic leg bouncing.

"What's the matter? Aren't you happy for me?" I was still beaming.

"Of course I am, but I want to go with you." He pouted. "Sarah, you're the first person since my parents were killed who gets me. What am I supposed to do now?"

Sitting next to him, I took his warm hand in mine. His palms were sweaty, and I could feel the vibration of nerves pulsating through his hand. "Robbie, if you do what they ask of you and stop rebelling, they'll let you out, too. Follow the rules, or at least pretend to. You have to try, or you'll be stuck here forever."

"Let's say that I do, and they let me leave. Will we be together? You and me, for real?"

Crap, I wasn't expecting that. The chances of me running into him again were next to zero, so I lied, "Of course." I put my arm around him. He leaned over and kissed me in response to my touch. Kissing him back was mechanical, but it gave him hope to fight for his freedom.

In the morning, I stood by the door with my enormous black suitcase in hand, champing at the bit to leave. When given the go-ahead, I walked out the double door, giving a quick wave to the nurses behind me, and glimpsed Robbie skulking in the background. I gave him a half-hearted grin, knowing I was leaving him more alone than when I met him.

When I came out, she was against the car, wearing her faded jeans and a purple paisley T-shirt. Her hair was in an off-center part, and sweeping curls flowed around her oval face. As usual, a cigarette dangled from her fingertips. "Come on, Curly Sue, let's blow this popsicle stand."

We spent the first leg of the trip in uncomfortable silence.

"Let's grab some lunch," she said with one hand on the wheel and the other on my leg. We pulled into a roadside diner with a blazing pink neon sign beckoning us to come in.

A server led us to a booth in the back with seats covered in red leatherette, the kind that sticks to the back of your legs during summer. A small jukebox was perched at the end. As I scrolled through the music selection, Mom grabbed my hand. "How are you doing, sweetie?"

"I'm okay. More or less." I shrugged, not making eye contact.

"Sarah, look at me," she insisted. "Honey, we need to talk about this. You nearly scared me to death. You know I had to be terrified to call your father for help."

"I'm so sorry, Mom, but I couldn't handle the agony anymore. I had nowhere to turn. There is no way you could ever understand." Subconsciously, I had shredded my napkin into tiny pieces of confetti.

"Actually, you're wrong. I understand entirely. I was in love once, and only once, for that very reason. When you're in love, it is the most fantastic feeling. It's as if you found this magnificent secret." Mom had a dreamy expression on her face, making me sit up a little straighter and listen a bit closer. "As euphoric as unconditional love is, the destruction it leaves behind is soul-crushing. I am so sorry you had to find that out the hard way. This is why I have always warned you not to let your heart get involved. Men leave. Granted, Jimmy didn't choose to go, but it wouldn't have worked, even if the accident didn't happen. The only people you can count on are Julie and me. Love is for fools and sweetheart, The Brennan Girls are no fools."

Chapter 6

WHEN WE PULLED INTO the driveway, I caught sight of Dad's new green Porsche parked on the street, and my body filled with dread.

"Honey, I am so glad you're home. I missed you." He grabbed me and held me tightly as I walked inside.

"That sucked," I spat out, breaking his grasp, and plopping down on our worn-out couch.

"Are you still mad at me?" His eyes dipped down at the corners. "You do understand that I did what I had to do. It was in your best interest."

"Whatever, Dad. I'm too tired to argue."

Being home was somewhat comforting in a way, but also had me confused. The future I had planned had changed in an instant. One innocent glance away from the road, and it was over. My dreams, Jimmy's life, and my childhood.

The four of us sat in a circle, staring at each other.

"Now what?" I inquired, breaking the silence.

"I think you need a little time to adjust to being home and how things are"—he hesitated—"now." Dad put his thick arms around my shoulder. "Oh baby, I'm so sorry all of this happened to you, but I promise you will be okay."

Any anger I held dissipated when I saw the sadness in his eyes. I dropped my head on his shoulder. "I know, Daddy. After I've had a few days to settle in, I'll readjust to life on the outside." I laughed at my own joke, but nobody else did. "I was thinking I may apply for a job or something in a few weeks or take a class at County."

"That sounds like a great idea. I'm proud of you, Princess. Let's chat again next week. I have to run. The little lady runs a tight ship. Love you." He kissed the top of my head and stood to leave.

As he walked away, I called out, "Hey Dad, what number is she?"

"Don't be a smart ass, Sarah," Dad chided.

"Sorry. Love you too."

Within seconds, the roar of his engine faded into the distance, and it was just The Brennan Girls once again.

Entering back into my bedroom was like slipping into a time machine. Our twin beds were still draped with the same matching pink floral coverlets. All the furniture was in the same place as when I left. I dragged my hand along the varnished top of our beat-up dresser and caught a glimpse of myself in the mirror. In the last few months, I had changed. Not only inside, but I appeared different; older, and wiser. Everything was the same, everything except for me.

Out of nowhere, Julie appeared behind me. I stared at her in the reflection. Her lips were long and thin, unlike mine, which were full and dusky pink. Her eyes were small and rodent-like; mine were wide-set and framed by thick Brooke Shields-like eyebrows. I wondered how two sisters could be so different?

"Hey Squirt, are you happy to have me home?" I continued to study our reflections in the mirror.

She wrapped both of her arms around my waist in a warm embrace. "I missed you. I was so worried. Sarah, please don't ever do that again."

"I won't."

"You have to promise," she insisted.

"Cross my heart and hope to die," I said with matching movements.

"Not funny," she cried.

Mom walked in looking like a million bucks, as usual. Her black wraparound skirt accented her tiny waist. The white polyester sateen shirt draped around her shoulder gave her a star-like quality, with her dark hair cascading over her full breasts. God, she oozed sex appeal.

"It's time to celebrate, Curly Sue. So put on your party dress, and let's hit the town." She did a snazzy little jig and smacked my bottom.

That was the first time Mom had invited me to go with her. It was a pivotal moment. I was about to find out what she did all those nights when she didn't come home.

I squeezed into my favorite acid-washed jeans, accented by a double-wrapped silver studded belt, and pulled on a black fishnet top over a black bra. Shiny silver hoop earrings and the silver high heels I had from graduation completed my outfit.

"What about me?" Julie whined.

"Moommm," I called.

Mom sat on the bed with Julie. "Sweetie, this is Sarah's welcome home present, and it's for grownups only. Why don't you have some friends over or watch one of those television shows you're always talking about? Most kids your age would love to be home alone."

"I'm not like most kids, or haven't you noticed?" Julie flopped back against the bed.

"Don't be a little snot, Julianne," Mom snapped back. "You'll be invited when it's your turn."

As Julie looked on longingly, I teased my hair, making it full, and sealing it with a healthy dose of Aqua Net and a squirt of Ciara behind each ear and one in my cleavage.

I was ready to hit the town to make my formal debut.

Chapter 7

THE FIRST SIX MONTHS at home were like living in an alternate universe. One where everyone was beautiful, and there were no rules. I spent most nights watching Mom sing at the nightclub in the hotel. As she belted out tunes, I sat upon my throne at the bar, with my obscenely long legs crossed, shoulders back, and a devil-may-care attitude. Scanning the smoke- and cologne-filled room, I eyed the businessmen unwinding after work, especially those sitting alone.

I learned how to spot a wedding ring from across a room, not that it was ever a deterrent. It's always good to know your mark. Closing in on my prey, I used all the arsenal that the master taught me. It was almost like a superpower, and it was intoxicating.

The ones who stared were not for me. They were too easy. Where was the fun in that? When I found one that piqued my interest, my legs swayed. Not quickly, as if I was nervous, but leisurely to the rhythm of the music. The tilt of my head and a sideways glance never failed to serve me. One deep sigh and he would be by my side.

"Hey, can I buy you a drink?" wondered Tony, the evening's entertainment.

I spun my seat to face him. Slowly, I ran the tip of my tongue across my lips, leaving them shiny and wet. When I uncrossed my legs, parting them a mere inch or two, I thought he was going to drop on the spot.

Now, that's fucking power, I thought.

His eyes darted from my lips to my breasts and to the dark path he knew led to a place that would make him beg for more.

"I have a better idea," I hummed, taking his hand. I led him out of the bar, glancing over my shoulder as I left, signaling to Mom that I was hunting. She acknowledged with a slight nod, only noticeable to the two of us.

I directed him to the ladies' room and slid the lock behind us. Grabbing him by his white starched collar, I pushed him against the wall, pressing my body firmly against his. He grew hard, and his member strained to break out of its prison.

"Do you like that?" I growled.

"Oh yeah, baby. I like that." He panted.

Hopping up on the counter, I raised my skirt, showing him my blatant lack of undergarments. One deep sigh, and he closed the gap. I unfastened his black leather belt. His trousers laid around his ankle as he reached into my top, grabbing my breast. He breathlessly took them into his mouth and greedily sucked.

"Easy tiger," I whispered, keeping control of the situation.

"Like this?" he teased, nibbling on the tender pink skin. My back arched, and I could feel myself growing wet and ready to welcome him.

"Yes, like that. Take me now."

He pulled me forward onto his stiffness, cradling my ass in his hands until we both climaxed.

"That was fun, Teddy." I patted him on the shoulder as I hopped off the cold linoleum and went into the stall to clean myself off.

When I returned, his lips were downturned, appearing distressed. "It's Tony. My name is Tony."

Mom and I would laugh to the point of tears on the ride home. We took turns telling stories of our latest conquests, shredding our poor victims who didn't know what hit them. After the encounters, sometimes I took their number, and we dated for a little while. Sometimes it was a one-and-done. So much depended on my mood and my needs at the moment.

As my twentieth birthday drew near, Dad had enough of the "shenanigans," as he called it, demanding I get a job. I supposed he was right. Adulting would have to happen, eventually.

While combing through the Sunday classifieds, I came upon a job I was qualified to do.

Wanted! Administrative assistant for small financial advisor. No experience required—competitive compensation and benefits. This week, interviews will be held; read the ad with a local phone number.

First thing Monday morning, I made the call and scheduled an interview. I showed up at the designated address in a burgundy skirt and mom's white sateen top that made heads spin and walked out with a job.

"Sarah, get over here," Mom bellowed from the living room, waking me up from a steamy, sexy dream.

"What the hell, Mom?" I yelled back. I dragged myself out of the covers wearing Jimmy's striped boxers and an old, stained white tank top and traipsed in to meet her.

On the counter sat the most elaborate basket I had ever seen. Fresh fruit, bagels, salmon, and chocolates teetered one on top of the other. You name it, and it was there.

My mouth began to salivate. "Where did this come from?" I asked, biting into a perfect red apple.

She handed me a little white card. The kind that comes when flowers are delivered.

Welcome to the team.
I am looking forward to Monday. -Stanley

"Who the hell is Stanley?" Mom asked with suspicion.

"My new boss. Wow, this is kind of wild. Want some?" I handed her a luscious pear, which she immediately smacked away.

"Sarah, this isn't normal."

"What's the big deal? He's a dorky little guy willing to pay me. I was lucky he gave me the job."

She was being annoying, as usual.

"Please, Mom, don't ruin it." I cut the conversation short by running back to bed and snuggling under the covers for another hour.

I spent the rest of the day shopping at the Livingston Mall with Julie for some suitable work clothes. We had a blast trying on things we couldn't afford, eating Burger King, and checking out guys. At times like that, I was grateful to have a sister.

The same screeching voice woke me the next day. "Sarah, come out here now." Mom's voice demanded.

"Damn it, Mom, what do you want now?" I muttered, leaning against the doorway, rubbing the sleep out of my eyes.

"Open your eyes, and you'll find out for yourself."

"Holy fucking shit! What the hell is that?"

"Mind your language. You will get nowhere if you sound like a truck driver," she scolded. "Now, explain this." She pointed to the dining room table.

Before me stood a three-tiered white wedding cake, topped with a plastic bride and groom.

"Was it delivered here by accident?" I was somewhat amused by the strange events of the week.

"Read the card that accompanied it," Mom demanded, with her arms tightly folded against her chest.

"Until the end of time, you will be mine, Stanley." Shivers ran up and down my body. "Oh my god. Mom, what is this?" I dropped the card on the floor as if it was in flames.

"I told you something was wrong. I have a sixth sense when it comes to men. This one is bat shit crazy." It was as if she could smell the danger. "You are not to work for this guy. Do you hear me? You call him right now and tell him something else came up."

"Yeah, of course. Can I still eat the cake?"

"Ha-ha," she snapped with nostrils flared and lips pursed.

I headed to the kitchen phone and called Stanley's office. The response I received was so chilly it could have made ice out of boiling water. I politely ended the conversation and hung up.

Two days later, a huge black stretch limousine pulled up in front of the house. I opened the curtains enough to peek out between the sheer cream-colored drapery. Out walked a dapper, middle-aged gentleman in a full black driver's uniform. He leaned toward the back and opened the door for its passenger.

Out came the bald little man with a warped sense of appropriate behavior.

I had nowhere to hide; he had already caught me peeking through the window.

I opened the door a crack. "Hi. What are you doing here?" The hair on my arms was standing on end.

"Hello, Sarah." He elongated the 's' and emphasized the 'ah' in my name. Uber creepy. He held a beautiful bouquet of exotic flowers bundled in purple satin ribbon. "These are for you. May I come in?" Before I could say 'no,' he shoved the door open and made his way into the living room.

"Uh, yeah. I guess," Every instinct told me to be extremely cautious.

Without hesitation, he made himself comfortable by sitting on the couch and patting the seat next to him.

Instead, I sat on the needlepoint wing chair we kept in the corner.

He swiveled in my direction. "Sarah, let me start by saying how disappointed I was that you didn't come to work with me. I think we would have made a fine team." He drummed his finger against his cheek. "Now that I've had time to mull our situation over, I think you were correct in turning down the position. This will allow us to pursue the relationship we are meant to have." He leered at me as he pushed up his silver, wire-rimmed glasses. He leaned slightly forward in my direction. "You feel the pull too. Don't deny it." His lips curled up at the corners, appearing like The Joker.

I tried to speak, but he quickly stood up and came toward me before I had a chance. He pressed his stubby finger over my lips. "Shh, now. I have a magnificent evening planned for us. Go put on your finest dress and come with me. We have lots to discuss." He took a long inhale of my hair and hummed with delight.

The invasion of my personal space made me grimace, but I tried to keep my voice steady and authoritative. "Stanley, I don't mean to be rude, but I'm not going anywhere with you. I apologize if you got the wrong message."

Tiny beads of sweat formed on his hairless head and his face turned stony. He took a deep breath and then released it as if he was blowing out a candle. His lips puckered until it was fully expelled. "I don't think you appreciate the gravity of the situation. Is this what you want?" He rubbed his finger against the molding and flicked at the dust in disgust. "I can give you everything... anything. You don't have to live like this anymore. Agree to cohabitate with me, and you can have your heart's desire. We can travel the world." The creepy smile was back again.

For a split second, my mind wandered to Paris. I envisioned myself strolling into a small boutique on the Champs-Élysées and trying on beautiful dresses. I could almost smell the croissants and coffee wafting in the breeze.

"Good, I see you're thinking about it." His voice oozed with satisfaction, and he took my hand.

That was enough to pull me out of my fantasy. "No, definitely not. Stanley, I don't want to be rude, but you need to leave, and if you come back, I will call the police."

He stood, straightening his suit jacket, and ran his fingers through what hair remained on the sides of his head. "Until we meet again." With a wink, he walked out the door. The screen door closed with a crack, and I fell back in relief.

My entire body was shaking. *This guy is a psycho*. Mom always taught us to use our spidey senses. If we suspected something was off about someone, we should always listen. Our bodies could pick up the vibrations of others, especially the crazy ones. I promised myself I wouldn't make that mistake again.

A little after midnight, the phone rang. I leaned over, grabbing the receiver before it woke Julie up. "Hello," I whispered.

"Sarah, is that you?" A voice questioned softly from the other end.

I sat up, still groggy from my sleep. "Yes, who is this?"

"It's Stanley," he whirred. "I understand you said you are unavailable to indulge in courtship at the moment, but I have something you ought to see, a fantastic gift. It will change the way you view the world forever."

"I told you, no. Do not call here again." I hung up the phone and unplugged the wire from the wall. "Creep," I uttered to myself.

I spent the rest of the night analyzing our previous encounters, wondering if I had done anything to lead him on. Of course, I was flirty at the interview, but that was just to get the job. All women do that. And yes, I hesitated when he mentioned France, but what girl wouldn't? My head spun as I replayed every word and every gesture until I finally drifted off.

Hours later, I awoke to my mother's panic-stricken face an inch above me. "Get your ass out of bed now! What have you done?" She kept her voice low. "The police are here."

"Mom, I swear, I didn't do anything." I pulled on the sweatpants that were lying on the floor and a baggy sweatshirt. We walked out arm in arm.

"Hi, Sarah. I'm Officer Donovan, and this is my partner, Officer Carlyle. Why don't you have a seat?" Reaching for the couch behind me, I lowered myself, not taking my eyes off their uniforms.

"I'll bet you're wondering what this is all about. Don't worry; you did nothing wrong." With that statement, Mom and I let out audible sighs simultaneously. "Last night, the Ramsey Police Department had a report of gunshots at a private residence. Upon entering, they found a man in his mid-forties with a self-inflicted gunshot wound to his temple, and they found a note on the table next to him. It's addressed to you." They handed me a transparent plastic evidence bag that held a cream-colored monogrammed piece of stationery.

My Dearest Sarah, I tried to tell you of my gift, the gift of eternal love. We could have been together for all time. It is with a heavy heart that I take my leave of this earthly plane and wait for you among the stars up in heaven.

Until we meet again,
Stanley

Mom grabbed the note, read it, and handed it back to the officers.

"Sarah, can you tell us what your relationship was with this man?"

I started at the beginning, told them everything that happened that week, and ended with the phone call in the middle of the night.

"What would have happened if she had gone?" Mom's voice quivered in advance of hearing the answer.

"Ma'am, we believe his intent was a murder-suicide."

Both officers looked my way. Then, the one with the beard said, "Good instincts, young lady. Make sure you always listen to your inner voice."

Chapter 8

I STARTED HAVING REOCCURRING nightmares after the Stanley incident, which is how we began to refer to it. In my dreams, Stanley had a gun to Jimmy's head, the silver barrel pressed against his temple. Stanley pulled back the hammer in slow motion, so I could hear the click of it locking into place. "So, Sarah, what's it going to be? If you come with me, he lives. If you don't, he dies. Your call, my darling." The Joker grinned.

Every night, I woke up in a cold sweat, with my heart ready to jump out of my chest. I was going mad from exhaustion. Picking up the phone, I dialed the number I etched in my heart. The phone rang four times before her heavy Long Island accent answered, "Ello."

"Hi, this is Sarah. Is my dad around?"

Shelly, wife number whatever, asked me to hold on as she hollered for him over the dishes clanging. I hated when she picked up. I never knew how to address her or what to say. On the other hand, she never tried to make conversation either.

There was a click as Dad came on the extension. "You can hang up now; I've got it," he yelled.

As soon as I heard his voice, my eyes stung with tears fighting to come out. "Daddy, did Mom tell you what that crazy bastard did?"

"Yes, Princess. She called me as soon as the police left. I'm so sorry I haven't had a chance to reach out, but Shelly's kids were here, and they are impossible."

"Yeah, whatever." I rolled my eyes, even though he couldn't see. "Dad, I need to get out of this God-forsaken town. Nothing good ever happens to me—first Jimmy and now this psycho. I need to start over somewhere. Can I come live with you? Please," I begged.

"That would be a negative, honey. You wouldn't be happy here. Personally, I would like nothing better, but Shelly would never go for it. She is especially moody these days. Did I tell you she's pregnant?"

"Nope. That's news to me." My insides began to churn, realizing that was why he didn't come running after the Stanley incident. "I suppose congratulations are in order. So, congratulations; now what should I do? I have to get out of here, like, pronto."

"Sweetie, don't worry. Give me a few days. I'm sure I'll think of something. Hang in there. How's Mom?"

"She's good. She's dating some married dude. He's a decent guy, always bringing us presents and stuff, but he's still married in the end. It's kind of messed up, don't you think?"

"Your mom is definitely not the conventional type. It's one of the things I always loved about her."

"I can't imagine you two all gooshy in love."

"Yeah, well, there is a lot you don't know about our relationship."

"Maybe we should keep it that way. Now, can we get back to me and what the hell I'm going to do next?"

Dad came through for me. He sent me a ticket to Arizona to visit the son of an old Army buddy, Larry, who owned a hotel in Sedona. Larry's father, John, was Dad's best friend when they were in the service. The two men were so close that they got matching tattoos of an eagle with its wings extended, the American flag in its talons, and USAF in an arch above the eagle's head.

The ticket came with the promise of a job and a place to stay. As soon as I got the news, I ran to the basement to grab the biggest suitcase we had. I threw it on my bed and began shoving in almost everything I owned until it was bursting at the seams. At last, I was going to head out west. It may not be the trip I had planned with Jimmy, but I was getting the hell out of Jersey and away from all the soul-sucking memories.

As I finished zipping it up, a muffled whimper came from the corner of the room. "Hey." I grabbed the pillow off her face and sat beside her. "What's the matter?"

"You're leaving; that's what's the matter. First Dad, then Grandma and Grandpa moved to California, and now you. Why does everyone leave me? Please, Sarah, don't go. I don't want to be here alone."

"First of all, Dad didn't leave us. He left Mom, and, well, she didn't give him much of a choice in the matter. We were the collateral damage. Second, Grandpa retired. He always wanted to live in San Fran, and you know that. He talked about moving whenever we saw him. It has nothing to do with you. And sis, I'm not leaving you. I'm going to find myself. There's a difference. I'll only be a phone call away if you need anything." I pulled my little sister into an embrace. "Now, it's time for you to start growing up. You aren't a baby anymore."

"Stop calling me a baby. God, you really have no idea who I am," she moaned with her brow furrowed. "Just go, Sarah. It's all about you. Everything is all about you. I hope you find what you're looking for." She threw her pillow at me and stormed out, slamming the door for good measure.

Another moment to add to the list of soul-sucking memories in Jersey.

Chapter 9

THE PLANE'S WHEELS TOUCHED down on the black tarmac with a jarring bump. All the passengers cheered and clapped, celebrating our safe arrival in Arizona. I was mixed with emotions. Part of me was beyond excited to have a fresh start. Still, another part of me was equally terrified of the unknown.

After deplaning, I scanned the unfamiliar airport, searching for anyone who looked like they were waiting for me.

A man, much younger than I had expected and strikingly handsome, held up a white sign with black lettering saying, 'Welcome to Arizona, Sarah Brennan.' He was tall, over six feet, with shaggy light brown hair and a thick mustache that brought to mind The Marlboro Man who graced many billboards along the New Jersey Turnpike.

As the distance between us lessened, I took note of his lopsided grin and straight white teeth shining through the furry caterpillar above his lip.

"Hey there, you must be Sarah. Your dad told me all about you, but he did not tell me you were such a knockout. Wowzah!" He burst out with no shame, grabbing me into a hug.

I blushed at the compliment. "Would it be safe to assume you're, Larry, or did I just hug a stranger?"

"I am a stranger, but also Larry. Let's go grab your luggage and head to the hacienda." We ventured off to the baggage carousel while exchanging pleasantries.

Larry hoisted my suitcase into the back of his black Jeep. The hard top was off, and the fenders were caked in red earthen clay. I hopped into the doorless car and settled in for the new adventure that was about to unfold.

As we drove, I kept glancing at the dimple in his chin and his aristocratically straight nose, while searching for something to say. "My dad doesn't speak much about his days in combat. He talks about his service days in general and the cool places he went, but none of the down and dirty stuff. He always seals up like a clam when I ask about it. Did your dad tell you any of the details?"

"Not much, but I know they saw some heavy shit go down. Dad still has nightmares. He's on a bunch of meds to keep him from losing his mind. Most of what he talks about is how your dad is the bravest guy alive."

"Yeah, he kind of is." I nodded in agreement.

Larry was obviously uncomfortable with the subject and quickly diverted my attention by playing tour guide. "Do you know why the rocks are red?" he quizzed, more rhetorically than expecting an answer. "The process is called iron oxide weathering. That means rust has turned the natural shale and sandstone red." He drove with one hand on the wheel and pointed with the other. "The plateaus and buttes surrounding us were caused by a steady water flow over thousands of years." It was as if we were driving through Mars with the dips and valleys all around. Red mountains jutted from the earth, but not sharply like a stalagmite with a pointy tip. They were enormous, with flat tops. In geography class, I learned they were called mesas because they were flat like a tabletop. He must have noticed how mesmerized I was by the sights surrounding us. "If you think this is something, you should be sure to go outside and see the night sky. The stars are so bright, you barely need headlights to drive, and shooting stars streak by constantly."

"I've never seen a shooting star." My voice was filled with excitement that I might get to see one in real life. "There are too many streetlights in Jersey to see much of anything outside the basics. You know, the moon, big dipper, and stuff."

Larry proceeded to tell me about the first time his mother showed him the milky way. When he was five years old, she packed up a picnic dinner and took him out to the Devil's Bridge. After their dinner of cold fried chicken and potato salad, they laid on a blanket as she pointed out the constellations. When she got to the milky way, he was devastated to find that the sky was not actually lined with candy bars. We both laughed at the innocence of youth.

"Hey, Larry. Why are the trees all twisted up? They look crazy."

"That is part of the magic of Sedona."

He pulled the Jeep over, jumped out, and waved for me to follow him. We walked up to a tree that appeared more like a sculpture than nature.

"See this? Notice how the trunk twists and curves. This is because of the vortex. Some say that Sedona is one of the most powerful energy-emanating spots in the world. They say the energy dances around like a tornado. Can you feel it?" Larry wondered, as he stroked the gnarled brown trunk.

"Maybe." I did sense a tingling on the back of my neck. Or perhaps it was the power of suggestion and all that jazz.

He winked at me when I didn't elaborate. "Come on. I want to make it back before dinner. Wait until you try the gastronomical magic of our chef. You will never want to eat anywhere else."

We jumped into the Jeep and went on with our journey.

In the distance, the cactus gave the illusion of people with their hands on their hips. The surrounding terrain was barren in some areas, while greenery sprang to life a mere stone's throw away. From deep within my soul, I knew it was the start of my autonomy.

After passing through a gatehouse, we pulled up to a compound comprising several adobe-style buildings. Before jumping out, a stout and jovial bellman, who clearly respected Larry, greeted us. "Good evening, Sir. How may I be of assistance to you?"

"Greg, this is my guest from New Jersey. Sarah will be staying with us for a while. Please take her bag and put her in the suite next to mine." He gave a wink in my direction. "I promised your dad I would keep a close eye on you."

We rode the elevator up to the top floor. There were only two doors along the long corridor. He slid the key into the door's lock closest to us and opened it wide, allowing me to take in the palatial suite all at once.

"How do you like the digs?" he asked.

"This is all for me?" My mouth was slack in awe. I had to make a conscious effort to close it.

"Yup, all for you, Chakita. The bathroom is on the other side of that door. If you open the sliders, there is a small Juliette balcony where you can catch the sun coming up. My room is right on the other side of that door. All you have to do is knock if you need me."

"This is amazing. How can I ever thank you?"

Our bodies both knew the answer to that question.

"Why don't you wash up and meet me in the lobby at seven for dinner?"

After Larry left, I stripped off my clothes. The bathroom held a deep soaking tub, which I filled with hot soapy water. I slipped in slowly, appreciating being enveloped in the warmth. Down, down, I went, submerging my head and body. Peering through the water, the room took on a wavey, surreal quality. I stayed like that until I had no breath left. Breaking back out, my laughter echoed in the pristine bathroom.

As I rinsed the soap off my legs, I noticed my fingertips were pruned, bringing back memories of swimming at my grandparents' house. Julie and I would stay in the water for hours, pretending to be beautiful mermaids hiding our secret from the world. Grandpa would yell out, "Girls, your lips are blue; let me see your fingers." At that, we would have to hold up both hands for inspection. If our finger pads were pruned, we had to get out. One time, Julie refused, and Grandpa chased her from one side of the pool to the other to capture her. He gave up after a few rounds. "You win, but don't you dare tell your grandmother." He waggled his finger. "She will have my head on a silver platter. You have five more minutes, little miss," he told her, feigning anger. Pruned fingers always reminded me of that day.

I climbed out of the bath and put on the fluffy white robe from the back of the door, embroidered with two intertwined maroon S's and an R for Sacred Space Resort.

After toweling off, I rifled through my suitcase. My clothes were flung everywhere, leaving a sea of cotton and polyester on the floor. I found a tie-dyed lavender sundress that wasn't too badly wrinkled among the avalanche. I wet my hands, wiping the creases away with some success, and then shimmied into the cotton sheath. I decided on the beige pair of Candie's sandals I bought that day Julie and I went shopping—for the job I never started. Next, I put my hair in a pearl banana clip and brushed my bangs down to soften my face. Carefully, I applied makeup, giving off the appearance of being older than my chronological age, but not slutty. Mom's ever-present voice echoed in my head, 'Sweetie, when you wear eye shadow, you want it to be smokey, sultry. If you cake on the chalky blue powder, people will think you're a hooker.' I used a deft hand as I was taught.

One last overview, and I was ready to go.

Chapter 10

STEPPING OUT OF THE elevator and into the bustling lobby, a parade of well-dressed guests milled about. The men held high-ball glasses filled with beige liquor. The ladies delicately held martini glasses adorned with olives.

I smoothed out my dress one more time, glanced in the silver of the elevator, and walked across the floor as nonchalantly as my body would allow.

When I arrived, Larry was in deep conversation with a man who had to be the maître d'. As I approached, Larry gave a quick wink that was meant for me alone. "Jean, this is Sarah; she will be helping you as hostess this season."

Jean stared at me through the thin-rimmed glasses perched upon his rather sizeable, bulbous nose. His paper-thin mustache twitched with disapproval. Larry gave him a piercing stare that was not to be refused.

"It is a pleasure to meet you, Miss Sarah," Jean addressed me formally with a tight jaw. "I look forward to educating you in the business of hospitality."

"Thank you, Jean. I am looking forward to it as well," I replied politely with a demure smile, trying to charm him with my good manners. Larry took me by the arm, escorting me to a small table in the corner of the room where we would be able to watch the dining room fill with smoke and a choir of chatter.

It amazed me that someone as young as Larry owned everything in sight, right down to the silver-plated sugar spoons. The room felt electric as well-groomed guests buzzed around, taking their seats at the formally set tables. The scene stirred up memories of the excruciating formal dinners with my grandparents in Manhattan. The difference being, here, I was allowed to speak. My grandmother was old school and ridiculously strict. Her favorite saying was, 'children are to be seen but not heard.' Julie and I were constantly chastised about our posture and table manners. Now, I wasn't the child. I was another adult in the room.

"Wow," I said without even thinking, as I watched the hustle and bustle of the waitstaff.

He blushed a little. "I'm extraordinarily proud of it. I worked hard to get here. Sometimes the staff thinks that I'm too much of a perfectionist"—he shook his head—"but that's only because it's not their money or reputation on the line. I built this place from the ground up. It's my baby."

"I get it. I promise I'll do an excellent job as hostess and will not disappoint." I crossed my heart and held out my littlest digit. "Pinky swear."

A gentleman arrived at our table with a tray of food that had not been ordered. Larry must have read the expression of confusion on my face. "We have what we call a prix fixe menu. What that means is that there are only a few offerings. This allows quality control and ensures all of my guests have a fantastic dining experience."

"Oh, what if the diner doesn't like what's on the menu?"

"We don't generally have those issues. Dietary restrictions are discussed beforehand. Why? Do you have any allergies or dislikes?"

"No, I was just saying," I tripped over my words.

Four brown and golden shells sat on a plate in a sea of butter and garlic that gave off a delicious scent. The clatter of my fork hitting the china made a terrible noise when I realized what was served.

"What's the matter? Do you not like escargot?" Larry asked, holding back a snicker.

With conscious control of my facial expression, I did not let my apprehension show again. "I'm not sure. I've never had snails before."

People around us ate them with silver tong and small fork. I followed their example. "Wow, these look really gnarly but taste amazing," I said, plucking each one out of its hiding place. Once I had eaten all the protein inside, I lapped up the garlic butter with the rest of the dinner rolls.

"I'm glad you like them." He was resting his cheek on his palm, staring at me.

"You're not eating? Is something wrong?" Suddenly, I felt self-conscious. I wiped my chin, thinking perhaps I had food on my face. I grazed my tongue over my teeth in search of stray food particles.

He placed his hand on top of mine. "Relax. Nothing is wrong. I'm enjoying you enjoying the food," he said with a hint of amusement in his voice. "Bon appétit." He raised his wineglass.

I raised mine as well, and we clinked, "Bon appétit," I cheered back and took a heavy swig of the crisp chardonnay.

We languished over our entrees of Chateaubriand with a rich red wine and earthy mushroom reduction, taking the time to appreciate each bite. The whipped potatoes were laced with a hint of truffle and garlic. It was possibly the best meal I had eaten in my entire life. The hours slipped by as we exchanged superficial stories of our pasts. Dad had told him about Jimmy and

Stanley when he made the arrangements. He did not know about the stint in rehab. I only deduced this from his not bringing it up. From what I was learning about him, he didn't seem the type to hold back.

His voice, stories, and sexy vibe enraptured me. My body automatically responded when he brushed against my skin. He said nothing aloud, but it seemed as if he was enjoying my delicate situation as I subtly squirmed in my seat. I had to remind myself I was a guest and shouldn't screw it up.

He and I walked back to my room in silence. Our hands lightly brushed each other as our arms swung. Once the key was in the door, I turned in his direction. Head tilt, hair strand, crooked smile. His response was as I had hoped. Grabbing me by the nape of my neck, he leaned my head back, exposing the hollow of my throat.

"Sarah, sweet Sarah, let me drink you in," he groaned longingly.

His hazel eyes twinkled in an array of browns, greens, and golds. My breath was catching in my chest. My head was saying 'no' while my body was saying 'Oh my god, yes.'

"We can't." I managed to sputter out.

"Sarah, it's not like we're related. Our dads are friends, and now we are. Let me in. Let me all the way in." His voice was seductive and impossible to resist.

I stumbled backward through the doorway with his arms still wrapped around me. He kicked the door shut and guided me to the king-sized bed without missing a beat. As we kissed, the spaghetti straps of my dress fell. His mouth traveled down my neck to my shoulder. He slid the dress down with one finger and continued his path. His lips danced on my hardened nipples, darting his tongue around them. He reached up under the skirt and slipped down my panties.

"Ah, beautiful Sarah," he murmured as he touched between my legs. "I see you want this too." He licked my dew off his fingers.

"I do. God help me. Yes, I do," I moaned.

Laying me down upon the bed and spreading my legs with his knees, he knelt on the ground. I gave no resistance. His tongue darted around my dark, warm spot while his finger explored me inside. I gasped as he demonstrated his expertise.

"Shall I keep going?" he teased.

"Please, don't stop," I begged, pushing his head back down. My hips raised to meet his probing tongue. The wave was rising through my body, until the crest was imminent.

"No, not yet," he whispered, stopping what was making my body tense with anticipation.

"Why? What are you doing? Don't stop."

"Not too fast. Let's let the anticipation linger. Why don't you finish for me? Let me watch."

Placing my hand between my legs, I finished myself off. After I achieved an orgasm that left me limp, he tucked me into bed with a kiss on the cheek. "This is going to be an amazing summer. Sleep well." With that, he left.

I lay there, unsure of what happened and what it meant. Was it a dream? No, I was almost positive it wasn't. I flipped over, drunk and sleepy. My mind drifted into that space between reality and dreams before welcoming the darkness.

Chapter 11

IN THE MORNING, I pressed the heels of my hands into my eyes, trying to remember and forget the details of the previous evening. My stomach was sour, my head foggy, and my bladder aching to be emptied. Pulling myself out of bed was accompanied by the groan that one would hear from an eighty-year-old man.

After I relieved myself, I glimpsed my reflection in the mirror. *You look like shit, girl.* I popped a couple Tylenol, stuck my mouth under the faucet to wash them down, gave each eye a healthy dose of Visine, and splashed some cold water on my face. The jangle of the bedside phone pierced through the silence as I was drying off. I dove across the bed to grab the telephone receiver.

"Hello," I answered breathlessly.

"Hello, honey. Did I catch you at a bad time?" asked Mom.

"Hey, Ma. No, I was in the bathroom." I scurried back under the covers.

"How's it going? Behaving?"

"Define behaving." I gave a mischievous chortle.

"You are there to recover. This is not a vacation or the dating game. Remember that."

"I know, Mom. So, what do you know about this Larry guy?"

"Sarah Caroline Brennan, do not tell me what I think you're telling me." When she used my full name, she was pissed.

"We didn't bump uglies or anything, but we got a little down and dirty." I giggled.

She once again took this as her cue to remind me of the evils of falling in love with a side lecture on contraception and drug use. When she was finished, she informed me that my sister was 'dying' to talk to me.

There was a momentary pause, then a click of the extension being lifted. "Mom, I got it. You can hang up now," Julie's familiar voice yelled out.

When we were sure Mom hung up, Julie began, "Hey, Sis."

"Hey, Squirt. What's going on?"

"Sarah, I'm freaking out. I lost my virginity to Bobby last night."

"Congratulations! Welcome to womanhood. Took you long enough," I said, poking innocent fun at her.

"Sarah, it wasn't in a good way. I didn't want to," her voice creaked.

I felt a sharp stab in my heart. "What happened?"

"Bobby and I went to a party. We both drank too much. We went to his parents' house, and I passed out on the floor. I woke up with him inside me." She was now sobbing.

"Oh, no. I am so sorry that happened to you, Squirt." She has always been so naïve about guys. Perhaps the time had come for her to understand the truth. "If it's any comfort, the same thing happened to Debbie sophomore year. I'll tell you the same thing I told her. Guys only want one thing, the dark wet place between your legs. You own that. Do you know how to turn the tables?"

"No. How?" she wondered.

"You become the huntress. You take control. Sex is sex. It doesn't have to be anything more than pleasure and control. It gives you a certain amount of power."

"I don't like this. Not at all. I hate men. I hate my life." The crying droned on, and my patience waned.

"For fuck's sake, Julie. Grow the hell up. This is the real world. If you would stop watching the Brady Bunch, you would realize that you are not Cindy fucking Brady. In fact, Cindy is undoubtedly on her knees sucking off Bobby when the cameras are off."

"Thanks, Sarah. Thanks for nothing." The phone slammed in my ear.

I hung up the phone and stared at the ceiling, regretting the Brady Bunch comment, knowing it was a dick move on my part. Julie lives in a fantasy world, and she is going to get crushed if she doesn't realize that the only person who will protect her is her.

A light rapping on the door adjoining mine and Larry's suites broke my train of thought. I crawled out of the covers, cinched my bathrobe tight, unlatched the chain, and unbolted the lock.

"Good morning, sleepyhead." Larry presented a coffee in one hand and a cheese danish in the other.

"Is that for me?" I was suddenly starving.

"Yes, in-deedy. Drink up. Like my dad always said, let's get while the getting's good."

"Where are we going?" I mumbled as I stuffed the danish in my mouth.

He made his way past me and plopped down in the chair adjacent to my bed. "If you're going to be an employee of Sacred Space, I need to give you a proper tour. You'll mainly work in the dining room, but you may have to field some questions. You will need to have full knowledge of our amenities and schedules."

"Okay, give me fifteen minutes, and I'll be ready." I gave him a little salute and took the coffee and danish off to the bathroom where I would make myself presentable. I returned washed, powdered, wearing the cutest denim cut-offs and a red and white striped tube top.

"Ready," I announced loudly, returning to the room to find him on the bed.

"Jesus, how the hell am I going to get anything done with you around? Let's get out of here before I strip you naked and have my way with you," he exclaimed, popping up and rearranging his noticeable excitement.

My head tilted slightly to the left, while I ran my fingers through my hair in a most casual, yet intentional way. A winsome smile spread across my face. "I'm ready when you are." The double entendre was left to linger in the air.

After a preliminary loop, we stopped at the stables. The long wooden structure was full of majestic horses with gorgeous manes—their tales swatting at the flies that dared to enter their stalls. I was close enough to see their ears twitch.

"Here, take this sugar cube and place it in the flat part of your palm," Larry instructed.

"I'm scared. Won't it bite me?"

"No, but you have to make sure your fingers are down, or he might confuse it with a carrot."

I did as I was told. I held my hand palm side up with my fingers arched downward. The horse lowered his head, delicately nibbling the treat out of my palm. Giggling like a schoolgirl, I begged, "Can I do that again?"

They introduced me to each horse and its handler. I stroked them along their noses, caressing the short, stiff hairs beneath my fingers. They whinnied in delight. As soon as we left, I wanted to return.

We jumped back into the Jeep to visit the various pools sprinkled throughout the resort, the tennis courts, and the sauna house inspired by ones found in Finland.

My brain was working overtime to store the onslaught of information. I hoped I was able to keep it all straight. But, more than that, I wanted to return to the stables.

As we approached the back entrance of the main pavilion, I took Larry's hand in mine. It felt like such a natural thing to do, but Larry abruptly pulled his away.

"I'm sorry. I didn't mean to...." My words trailed off in embarrassment.

"No worries. I was surprised, that's all." His voice was tender. "Listen, it's kind of hard being the boss. I have to keep up appearances and don't want anyone to think I'm favoring you."

"Yeah, no problem." I tried to shake off my embarrassment and act nonchalant. "Larry? Do you think I could learn to ride? The stables were amazing."

When he nodded yes, his hair shook, so strands fell in his eyes. *God, he is handsome*. Suddenly, the memories of the previous night returned in a flood. It wasn't a dream. *Oh no, what am I doing?* I chastised myself. *Sarah, he is not your boyfriend. Don't be an idiot.*

Intellectually, I understood that what I was doing was dangerous and could jeopardize my position. Still, the more time I spent with him, the sexual tension increased. At least for me, it did. I realized he had been speaking while I was lost in my thoughts and only caught the last part of what he was saying. "Of course, silly. It's one of the perks of working here. You are free to use any of the facilities on your days off if guests don't book them."

"That is fucking awesome." The curse tumbled out before I had the chance to catch it.

I must have turned red because the next thing out of his mouth was, "Hey, no worries. If guests aren't around, you don't need to watch your P's & Q's. I'm not your dad."

You can say that again. You are so extremely fuckable. Aloud, I said, "Thanks, I have a bit of a gutter mouth, as my mom likes to call it."

But neither Larry's fuckability nor my gutter mouth would ruin this opportunity for me.

Chapter 12

EVERYTHING ABOUT BEING IN Sedona and the ranch resonated with me. I had never been particularly good at anything, but I was killing it in the dining room.

My position as hostess began with the basics of making sure the dining room was set correctly. Each place setting comprised a large white dinner plate with a smaller one on top—bread and butter plate off to the side. Two forks—sometimes three depending on the menu—were placed on a crisp white linen napkin. One spoon and a knife flanked on the right. Each table had a fresh floral centerpiece daily. For the evening meals, candelabras were added.

Within days, my responsibilities grew. Apparently, I had a knack for remembering our guests' names as well as their vices. I knew when Mr. Patterson needed a fresh bourbon with muddled fruit or when Mrs. Crawley wanted an extra piece of chocolate cake. Their wishes were fulfilled without anyone saying a word; everything would appear as if by magic. I walked around with my back straight and a welcoming smile, as if I were the leading lady in a play. Jean no longer treated me as if I was a brainless dolt. On the contrary, he often smiled at me and tipped his head with approval.

On my first day off, I woke up early and put on my favorite pair of jeans with the frayed hole in the knee and my new Sacred Space Ranch and Spa T-shirt that came with the job. I left out the employees' door and headed over to the stable.

"Hello," I called out. "Anyone here?"

A deep, scratchy voice answered my call. "Over here, little lady." Out stepped a burly man with white whiskers that covered most of his face. His chocolate brown leather hat sat on the rear of his head, making the front tip up like a sail on a boat. He appeared as if he had stepped out of a western movie. "What can I do for ya?" He looked me up and down with suspicion.

"Hi, you must be Bronco. My name is Sarah. I'm working at the ranch now." I extended my hand toward him, but he left it dangling in the air. Shoving them into my pockets, I continued, "Larry told me I could ride today if there weren't any guests booked. I peeked at the ledger and didn't see anyone scheduled. Would it be okay if I rode?"

"Do you have any experience? You don't look much like the riding type," he snarled, his lip bulging with chew.

"I was hoping you might teach me. I'm a pretty quick study."

"Hmm," he murmured with one eyebrow arched in what can only be described as skepticism.

"Is there a problem?" I was unable to hide my annoyance.

"No problem at all. You're a bit skinny to be a cowgirl, but if the boss man says you can ride, who am I to stop you?" He spit in the can he was holding. "First, go in the tack room and get yourself some proper shoes. If a horse steps on yer toes in those little white tennis shoes, they're gonna splinter."

I shuffled over in the direction he pointed. The tack room had dozens of boots of various sizes. I supposed they were for the guests. On the wall hung leather bridles and saddles that gave off a bouquet that was musty and rich. I found the aroma comforting. Standing up, I stomped my feet down on the straw-covered floor to ensure they were snug in the leather boots I had selected. Then, shimmying my shoulders to loosen up, I walked out, ready to take on the challenge ahead.

"Ya, look good there, Miss Sarah. We may make a cowgirl out of ya, after all. Come on over here; I want you to meet Star. Star is one of the gentlest beasts God has placed on this here Earth. She loves new riders and is real patient."

I cautiously held my hand out and brushed her white nose. "Hey there, Star. Would it be okay if we became friends?" She neighed as if to answer.

Both Bronco and I laughed.

The stall opened with a creak. Bronco showed me how he saddles and puts the harness on the horse. Once she was ready, Star and I followed Bronco onto the dusty beige pathway leading to the paddock.

"Jesus Christ, lady, never stand behind a horse. Are you daft or something?" Bronco loudly reprimanded me.

"Oh my god. What? What?" I called out, jumping away.

"Horses kick and kick hard if they get spooked. You always walk to the side or in front," he barked.

"I'm so sorry. I didn't know," I fretted, expressing my ignorance.

His brash demeanor softened a bit. "Listen, Missy, sorry for yelling, but I have witnessed too much in my days here at the ranch. I can see I have to start with the basics. Rule one: never, ever walk behind a horse. Got it?

"I swear I will not walk behind a horse ever again," I spluttered and felt a flush creep up from my feet all the way to my face. "I know nothing about horses or the outdoors. I was brought up in nightclubs. The wilderness for me is the Jersey shore."

Bronco grabbed Star's brown leather reins and walked her around the oval paddock while giving me the essential do's and don'ts of being around a horse and riding. After about twenty minutes, he allowed me to put my newfound knowledge to work. I placed my left foot into the stirrup, held onto the horn of the western saddle, and hoisted myself up and over onto my new friend's back. Star shivered with approval.

"This is so amazing," I squealed with delight.

"Now, give a little pressure with your thighs. It's kind of like tapping on the gas. If you give her too much force, she will run. Give her just enough to signal you want to stroll, nice and easy like."

Slightly pressing my knees closer to Star's sides, she plodded slowly. Her ears twitched away the flies, and her tail gently swung back and forth. I hardly had to do anything.

"Now sit back," yelled out Bronco. "That's it. Move with her. It's like swaying to music."

My new friend knew exactly what she was doing. I relaxed into the saddle, and we strolled out the paddock gate, up around the old cactus that reminded me of a gunslinger at the edge of the property and back. The air smelled of sunshine and rain simultaneously. I later found out the fragrance of precipitation is caused by a bush called creosote. The wonders of Arizona continued to reveal themselves like magical, unexpected presents.

As we traveled, my body relaxed into a natural cadence with Star. We moved as one unit. Our connectivity was calming and gave me a sense of peace. It was almost a religious experience. I was one with nature, beast, and God.

Chapter 13

LARRY AND I PLAYED a little more cat and mouse as the summer progressed, but we fizzled out once the novelty wore off. I think we both lost interest. And if I am being honest, I wanted to spend my time at the stables.

Star and I would see each other whenever I had an hour to spare. It was as if I was sneaking off to see a lover. If I didn't have time for a ride, I would take a few minutes to visit her in her stall and brush her long, white mane.

"Hey, baby girl. How are you today?" I spoke to her as I would any person. Of course, she didn't answer back with words, but she would whinny in response.

"I wish you could talk to me. My mom called yesterday. She says she wants me to come home, but I think I'm happy for the first time in my life," I said, pulling the soft brush down her back. "Oh, Star, what am I going to do?"

No one had cleaned her stall yet, so I grabbed a pitchfork and bucket. When I saw Bronco muck a stall the first time, I almost gagged as he scooped up the warm, steaming feces and plopped it into the green container with the ranch's logo on the side. I can't wipe my ass without being grossed out, but as time passed and Star became more than 'a horse', I didn't mind. I suppose the same thing happens when someone has a baby. It becomes something you do to comfort someone you love.

Glimpsing the clock at the rear of the stable, I realized I had lost all track of time, as I often did when visiting the barn. With a quick goodbye to Bronco and the horses, I bolted back to the main house to shower for the dinner shift.

I threw my hair up in a bun and tossed on a navy blue and white polka dot Diane von Furstenberg wrap dress I had bought in town the week before. Once I had money and a respectable job, my wardrobe escalated accordingly. The addition of navy espadrilles that wrapped at the ankle, not unlike ballet point shoes, and my favorite silver hoop earrings, completed the ensemble. Voila, presto change-o.

When I strolled into the dining room, I found Jean had his head buried in the reservation book as usual. Coming up from behind, I whispered in his ear, "Hey, handsome," in a mock flirtation.

"Hello, Miss Sarah. May I say you look magnificent this evening?"

"I bet you say that to all the girls." I winked and went on with my duties. As I walked around the dining room, I straightened the crooked silverware, plucked wilted flowers from vases, verified all candles were lit, and confirmed each chair was tucked in uniformly. When I was satisfied, I stood at the rear of the room against the panoramic windows with an unobstructed view of the unspoiled terrain. Surveying the space filled me with a sense of pride. This was my restaurant, my home. I couldn't imagine going back to New Jersey. Not now. Maybe not ever.

Chapter 14

TOURIST SEASON WAS COMING to a close as the cool air of fall crept in. It wasn't that the weather changed all that much. It was that life outside of the hospitality industry slowed after the summer rush everywhere.

All the staff quickly and efficiently went about their business on August twenty-third, the date when we would be told if Larry would be keeping us on. Jean informed me that Larry would be meeting with me at four o'clock. Watching the clock move in slow motion was torture. My insides felt as it was crawling with ants, making me want to escape from my own skin.

As I was making my way to the boss's office, Jean grabbed my wrist as I walked by, giving me a little squeeze, which hinted that he may have known something I didn't. Before knocking on the ornate walnut door with his name engraved on a bronze placard, I checked myself in the mirror on the opposite wall. I needed to use all my resources so Larry would let me stay. I reached into my bra, tugging at my breast to enhance my cleavage, and licked my lips, leaving them wet and dewy. Tentatively, I wrapped my knuckle against the door.

"Come on in," he called from the other side.

I sat in a small brown armchair directly across from him. For the first time, he gave the appearance of a boss, which I found intimidating. Larry held his position in the oversized leather chair, tidying up whatever paperwork sat before him.

"Hi, Larry," I let out a long sigh that didn't mask the tremble buried within it.

"Hey, Sarah," he spoke my name quietly. His eyes darted away from me as he continuously clicked the retractable pen he held in and out. When the clicking stopped, the air was still and silent, making me more anxious.

"I thought I was the one who was supposed to be nervous," I joked, hoping to ease the tension. "Whatever you have to say, Larry, I want to thank you so much. This was the most amazing summer I've ever had. Who would have thought that I would be running a dining room at a five-star spa in Arizona at my age? Especially after everything that has happened in my life." My heart was full of genuine gratitude and extraordinary sadness, knowing I was at the end of the most incredible journey.

"I'm thrilled to hear that, Sarah. You have been a real asset to us here at SSR. I've watched you grow into the hostess position and become a cowgirl. It has been an incredible transformation, and I'm glad you came to us. That being said, our clientele drops by over sixty percent in the fall. As much as you help in the dining room, it is Jean's domain. He has been here for years and has seniority." The edges of his mouth turned down, revealing that it pained him to have to let me go.

The tears welled up in my eyes without spilling out.

He continued, "I'm sorry, but we can't keep you on. It is nothing personal. It is purely a financial decision. I hope you understand."

Once the first tear escaped from the corner of my eye, a thousand more followed. Larry rounded his desk and took me in his arms. My body convulsed with emotion, and I pressed my face against his chest. He smoothed my hair with his fingers, soothing me almost like a child. Once I settled down, he whispered, "One for the road?" seducing me with his lust-filled eyes.

"Sure, why not?" With that, he locked the door and began kissing me. I fell into the rhythm of our bodies as if on automatic pilot. At least I knew how this would end.

We lay on his office floor, my head upon his chest. I played with the trail of hair that ran from his navel to his pubic region, absentmindedly.

"What are you thinking about?"

"I'm trying to decide what to do next. I have nowhere to go, and I don't want to go home."

"I'm so sorry, beautiful. Listen, you have a few weeks to figure it out. I will help in any way I can."

"Thanks, Larry. You have been a terrific friend and not a bad lay, either." I chuckled, trying to add some levity to the situation.

"Not bad?" He feigned anger. "Not bad, you say?" He held my wrists down and began kissing my breasts, and we were at it again.

Chapter 15

I WOKE AT FOUR on my last morning, aware that I would be back home sharing a bedroom with my little sister by nightfall. I threw on my riding jeans, my SSR T-shirt, and what had become my favorite red and black checked flannel. My boots sat by the door, scratched, and banged up. So much had changed since the day I purchased them.

After my second trip out to the barn, I understood that to be taken seriously, I would need to look the part if I wanted to ride. I had a couple hundred bucks sitting in the bank from my recent paychecks and treated myself to a shopping spree. I grabbed one of the Jeeps and headed into town. That was where I bought clothes for work and play. Horseplay, that is.

The boots came up to my mid-calf. They weren't like the cowboy boots one sees in movies. Instead, they were a rough brown with a thick bronze buckle outside the ankle and leather loops on either side to pull them on. The first time I took them out of the box, the aroma of fresh rawhide was explosive.

I grabbed my now worn boots and set out to the barn. I wanted to arrive before anyone else. As I made my way, I stopped and stared up at the sky. Millions of stars danced in the cloudless morning. I closed my eyes, making a wish on the brightest one. "Starlight, star bright, first star I see tonight. Wish I may wish I might have the wish I wish tonight."

The barn door creaked open, sounding like an alarm in the silence of the still air. Once inside, I smiled at the sight of my fair-haired beauty. Second stall down, her head peeked over her gate, as if she sensed I was coming.

"Hey girlfriend, were you expecting me?" I whispered, kissing her on the nose. "How about I saddle you up, and we take an early ride?" I stroked her neck, letting my body lean into her. She leaned back. The pressure of her weight countered mine. It was almost as if she knew this would be our last dance. On my way to the tack room, I caught someone lurking in the corner. "Who's there?" I called, attempting to sound tough but scared witless. Out of the darkness came a familiar outline. Stocky, once muscular, with his hat tipped back just so. "Oh, it's you." My nerves immediately settled back down.

"Nice greeting, girlie." His rough guffaw gave away that he wasn't actually annoyed. "I had an inkling you would be here today." He walked over and extended his hand. "We're gonna miss you 'round here, you city slicker. Especially that little lady over there." He motioned at Star with his chin.

"I'm going to miss you too, stud." I elbowed him gently in the ribs. "Would you mind if we go out for a ride before everyone wakes up?"

"Not at all. You go on. Take your time. I've got you covered."

"Thanks," I said while grabbing Star's worn saddle. I breathed in the familiar leather and hoisted it onto her back.

With the expertise of a seasoned rider, I mounted Star with ease. I settled into the smooth dip of the seat, leaning my lower back against the cantle. With a slight squeeze of my knees, we were off on our journey to nowhere.

We started with a loop around the resort, taking in the details of all the buildings. Through the dining-room window, the 'Exit' sign glowed into the vacant space. Not a single guest was stirring. The only noise was the clip-clop of Star's hooves and the whirring song of the cactus wren. It felt like yesterday I was the new kid in town. A longing settled into my heart, and I hadn't even left yet.

Next, we curled up into the trails to a ridge. The dusty red path led us to the canyon's far side, known for its fantastic sunrise views. The initial steep incline gave way to a narrow path with scrub all around. Star kept her gait steady, not once faltering, even when we arrived at the rockiest part of the trail. Up and up, we climbed until we reached the crest in time to see the sky turn from black to blue. Then melt into orange, pink, and yellow, like the colors of sorbet. No painting or photo in the world could ever do it justice. The pageantry of the dawning of a new day was intoxicating. Once the morning light covered the land, it was time to return.

"Listen, Star," I said, patting her on the side of her neck, "you are the best thing to ever happen to me. I wish you understood how much I love you."

She responded with a bray and a shake.

"That's right, girl; this sucks." I kissed my hand, transferring it gently to her neck. "We better get going."

As we approached the part of the trail with the steep decline, I leaned further back into my saddle, ensuring to not bring too much weight up front. Star took her time to find her footing. We were in our groove, moving as one. My peace was broken by the sound both visitors and residents dread—the shake of the Rattler. I spied him curled under a red clay rock. I kept my eye on him as we passed. Quicker than I could react, the snake darted out in front of Star, spooking her. She took to her hind legs to pounce on the viper. I toppled over, landing on the hard earthen ground with a heavy thud.

"Sarah, are you okay?" Larry's voice was filled with concern.

"Larry? Is that you?" I opened my eyes slowly. The glare of the sun was making my head scream.

"Yeah, it's me. When Star showed up without you, I knew something had to be wrong. How's your head?"

I rubbed the area that was throbbing. Bringing it back, I checked for blood, but it came back clean. "It hurts like hell, but it's my leg. I'm afraid to look."

"Let me see." He leaned back to survey the damage. Without delay, he whipped out his walkie-talkie. "Station house. This is Larry Kincade out at the SSR. We need the EMTs out on the ridge ASAP. It looks like a compound fracture of the right tibia and a possible concussion."

They brought me back down on a gurney carried by two enormous guys in their mid-twenties. When we reached the bottom, they hoisted me into the waiting ambulance. Everyone piled in. The sirens and lights cleared the way to the hospital.

Chapter 16

As THE GURNEY BARRELED into the emergency room, the bright lights, the overpowering smell of disinfectant, and people screaming hit me all at once. The sensory explosion was like a lightning bolt careening through my body. As soon as it hit my stomach, I threw up on the orderly's feet. The twisting action of trying not to puke on myself was excruciating.

I propped myself up and gasped at the sight of a jagged white shard protruding through the skin. "Oh my god, is that my bone?" I shrieked in horror.

"It's not as bad as it seems. You need to remain calm." The young nurse, who appeared not much older than I, tried to convince me. She lightly pressed my shoulders so that I would lie back down. "I need you to stay still so I can put in an I.V. Once that's in, I can give you some medicine to ease the pain. "

The young nurse moved methodically, wiping my arm with alcohol and inserting the needle in one attempt. Within minutes, the numbness took over. I was awake and still hurt, but the pain was removed from my consciousness. I was floating in a blissful disconnectedness.

"How's that?" the nurse asked a few minutes later.

"So much better. Thank you. Can someone call my parents?"

"It's already been done," said Larry. I hadn't seen him standing less than a foot away.

"Hey. Wow, that was messed up. How's Star?"

"She's safe and sound in the barn. She may have saved your life. What happened?"

I explained the story the best that I could. "We do have rattlers, but it's unusual for them to come out from their hiding place. I'm glad you didn't get bitten." He gently stroked my forearm, the only place that didn't look like it had been through a meat grinder.

"Me too." I chuckled, somewhat lightheaded.

"Listen carefully, Sarah. You saw your leg, right?"

"Yeah, dude, that is some disgusting shit," I blurted out, sounding like a stoner. "Shhh, Larry, come closer. Don't tell anyone, but I am so wasted. This shit rocks." I laughed hysterically.

His eyebrows were knitted in concern. "I'm glad you aren't in any pain. What I'm trying to explain is that you need to have surgery. They're coming to get you now. Your mom and dad should be here by the time you wake up."

"Mom and Dad together. This should be fun."

Orderlies dressed all in white came to wheel me to the operating room. Before leaving, I shouted out, "Rock on with your bad self," as I pumped my fist into the air. That was the last thing I remember until I woke up the next day.

Opening my eyes felt like daggers pushing into my brain. It was the worst hangover I had ever had. I called for a nurse by pressing the red button near my hand. The tall brunette on-call nurse arrived instantaneously.

"Hello. You're awake." She smiled down at me. "Your parents will be thrilled."

"They're here?" I murmured in a groggy voice.

"Yes, they arrived a little while ago. How is your pain level?"

"A ten. My head is killing me, and I can't feel my leg."

"Not to worry. I will get you some Tylenol with codeine for your head. That will knock it right out. As for your leg, we had to do a nerve block. It will wear off in a couple of hours, and then we will do our best to keep you comfortable with some more narcotics. Sarah, this was not a run-of-the-mill break. The surgeons had to put in two plates and several screws to put the bone back in alignment."

"I will walk again, won't I?" I was terrified she would say no.

"Of course you will." She gave my hand a pat that was meant to be reassuring. "You'll need to do physical therapy, but you will mend, not to worry. I've got to go. Press the red button if you need anything, and someone will be here in a jiffy." She smiled down at me while fluffing my pillow. "I'll be back with your meds soon."

Chapter 17

"Wakey, wakey, sleepyhead."

I felt someone combing through my hair.

"Come on, Curly Sue, it's time to open your eyes."

"Mommy!" I whimpered as if I was a little girl again. "Oh, Mommy, I'm so glad you're here." Mom looked years older than when I left, and her breath reeked of coffee and stale cigarettes.

"Hush now, sweetie. Mommy's here and look who else."

"Daddy."

My parents were far from perfect, but they came, and I was extremely grateful to have them with me.

"Of course, I'm here. You're my Sunshine." He squeezed my hand, giving me our secret signal. Three squeezes, for three words: I love you. I did the same in reply.

The surgeon walked in with a no-nonsense demeanor. His brown tortoiseshell glasses covered half of his face, and a gray handlebar mustache had taken over the lower. He made no formal introduction and only gave a brief overview of the surgery. Next, he explained to the three of us my recovery would be long and painful, but eventually, I would regain all normal function if I played by the rules. The information was decidedly clinical, devoid of human emotion, and then he was gone.

"I guess becoming an Olympic gymnast is out of the question." I chuckled.

"What a sour puss he is. Such a stick up his ass," Mom blurted.

"Boy, you girls are a brutal audience," Dad retorted.

"Excuse me, you were the one making goofy faces behind his back," I pointed out.

"Guilty." He threw his hands up in mock surrender. "He was so morbidly dry."

We started giggling again.

Once the laughter died down, Dad set a plan in motion. It had already been decided that Mom would stay with me until the hospital said it was safe for me to be moved. Then she and I would fly home, where I would begin physical therapy.

Dad would be returning to his other family that afternoon. Apparently the new baby had colic, his wife was crying all the time, and the world stopped revolving unless he was there to make everything all better. They had him totally whipped.

By the time I got home, I had become good at maneuvering on crutches. I was unexpectedly happy to be back in our little brick ranch. It hadn't changed a bit in my absence. Even the same musty smells hung in the air.

Mom held the door as I hobbled inside. A huge banner stretched across the living room made from an old white bedsheet that read, 'Welcome Home, Sarah.' Julie was standing underneath with a bouquet of wildflowers.

"Welcome home, Sarah." She approached me cautiously. "Is it okay if I hug you?"

"Of course, Squirt. Come on over here." As we embraced, I buried my nose in her hair, breathing in the Herbal Essence conditioner she used. It reminded me of home, of her—my sister.

"Here, let me help you to the couch." She held out her arm.

"I'm good," I assured her. With a few pushes of my crutch, I settled into our old, tattered couch. "Jul, can you do me a favor? Go in my purse and get the two prescription bottles. My leg is throbbing from the long flight."

"On it." She saluted and came back within seconds.

"One more thing, grab me a glass of water too, please?"

"You got it." She flew out of the room to fill my request.

While she was gone and Mom was making herself a scotch, I poured two Tylenol with codeine and a Percocet into my hand. I cheeked two pills so Julie and Mom would only see the one I held.

Julie returned with the water and what was obviously a forced expression of ease. "So, tell me everything. Don't leave out any details." She scooched up close to me, waiting to be regaled by my adventures.

Once the pills slid down my throat, I told her as much as made me comfortable and enough to keep her from hounding me. The recitation ended with the snake accident. By the time I reached the part about the hospital, the pills had begun their desired effect. The ethereal disconnect had returned. Bliss.

"Jul, I'm exhausted. I'm going to hit the hay." I pushed off on her thigh to stand.

"Totally. I totally get it. I'm so relieved you're okay. I really missed you." She stood up and hugged me before I left.

"I missed you too, Squirt."

I propelled myself into our room and lay on my bed to enjoy the high. Everything was so much more enjoyable while stoned. Television was funnier, people more interesting, and food more delicious.

Hours ticked away while I lived in a world that didn't hurt, physically or emotionally. My thoughts drifted in circles, trying to make sense of life's tragedies. So many people walk around with rainbows and butterflies shooting out of their asses. Dumb shits. Let's face it, life sucks, and then you die. With that thought, I drifted off.

My favorite white cotton blanket was covering me when I woke up, and my leg was propped on a pillow. Leaning on my elbow, I took two more T3s and swung myself out of bed.

I hobbled to the kitchen to find mom drinking a steaming cup of coffee. "That smells delicious, Mom."

She poured me a mug, adding a dash of milk and two spoons of sugar.

"Where's Julie?"

"She's at school. Senior year. Can you believe it? She's almost grown up."

"Yup. Being an adult is awesome. Not." My voice dropped a couple of octaves.

"Oh, stop being such a curmudgeon. Now that The Girls are back together, let's go out to celebrate in Brennan style." Mom wiggled her eyebrows and snapped her finger.

"Love to Mom, but first I have to be able to walk." I held out my cast, reminding her I was in no shape for anything, especially picking up guys.

"Fine." She glowered with the pout of a five-year-old. "But as soon as you're better, it's you and me against the world."

Chapter 18

THE DAYS DRONED ON endlessly. It was as if the world had stopped orbiting. The ranch, Larry, and Star were lost in some kind of space-time continuum. My life was a series of never-ending days of sitting around and watching television on our lumpy old couch while the rest of the world rolled on with their lives.

At night, my dreams became a taunting of things gone awry. *Jimmy is back and walking toward me. His smile is like the sun, warming my chilled bones. As he comes closer, his blue eyes become the night sky with shooting stars streaking through them. He starts mouthing words that I can't hear. Suddenly, I am sitting atop Star. I try to coax her into moving closer to Jimmy, but she firmly stays where she is. I beg her to walk, kicking at her sides, to no avail. I can't get down because she grows over twenty feet tall. Jimmy bridges the gap between us, still sparkly and shiny, but Stanley appears with a silver handgun, places it at Jimmy's temple, and fires three shots in succession while laughing his sinister laugh. Star's beautiful white coat is covered in dark red blood and blotches of Jimmy's brain. The ground below us begins to creak and groan as it shifts. The floor cracks open, becoming a giant abyss that swallows us up, and we tumble endlessly into the darkness.*

I was finally cleared to begin physical therapy. The surgeon wasn't kidding about how much my recovery would hurt. Still, with the help of my pills, I was able to put more and more pressure on my foot until I could walk again.

It took a solid six months to get rid of the limp. When the scars began to fade and the discomfort subsided, I tried tapering back on the pills. With each failed attempt, my heart would race, and I would break into a cold sweat.

One day, when I woke up from a nap, I couldn't feel my feet. It was as if someone had removed them in my sleep. I screamed, unable to move. "My feet! Mom!" I started crying. Now I was sitting up, banging on my uncooperative legs that lay under my covers like limp rags. "Someone, please help me!" I shouted, panicked by my paralysis.

"What is it, Sarah?" Julie came crashing into the room. "What's the matter? I could hear you all the way in the basement."

"My feet. I think they're gone." I sobbed. "Go tell Mom. Someone stole my feet."

"What are you talking about?" Julie flung back the covers. "Your feet are right here."

I peeked between the fingers covering my eyes. My two feet were attached to my ankles where they had always been, red toenail polish and all. I flopped back against my pillow. "I'm so sorry, Julie. I must have had a nightmare. Go on back to whatever you were doing." Seeing the terror on my sister's face made me realize that I may have taken too many pills. I have no doubt Julie understood what was happening because before she left the room, she flipped me the bird and slammed the door behind her.

I grabbed the handset and punched in his numbers with my trembling finger.

"Hello," his gruff voice answered.

"Hi, Daddy. It's me." Tears sprang to my eyes. "Daddy, I messed up. Can you come and help me?"

I stayed held up in my room. I didn't want to speak to Mom or Julie about what was going on. Mom would likely ask if she could have a pill and then offer to take me out partying, and I was sure Julie would be useless in that particular situation.

In the morning, he arrived in my room. His icy blue eyes were red from driving all night. "Hey there, sunshine. How's my girl?" he asked. I don't think he suspected, but I came clean and told him everything. He was the only one I trusted to look out for my best interest.

"You understand you have to go back, right?" It was more of a statement than a question.

"I do, but I don't want to, Daddy. I'm so sorry I screwed up." My remorse was genuine, but so was the pull to get high.

He held me close. "This is not your fault, sweetie. Someone should have been monitoring your meds closer. Someone like your mom."

"It's not her fault, Daddy. It's mine. I hid what I was doing. I'm so sorry."

"Why don't you pack your bags? I'll send Julie to help. Okay?" he said, kissing me on top of my head. Then he placed his warm, reassuring hand on my back. "Get a hurry on. I have to get back home."

Julie came in with a suitcase in tow. "Where are you going this time?" She tossed the black bag at me.

"I'm going back to rehab." I averted my eyes to the gray shag carpet in shame.

"Way to go," she said between tight lips and gritted teeth. "What, were you missing having Dad's attention, or was life not dramatic enough? It's always something with you. I am so sick of it!" Her features were twisted, and her fists were bouncing off the side of her legs in tight balls.

"Fuck you," I muttered loud enough that only she could hear.

"Why don't you go back to Arizona and trick some dumb ass into marrying you? Or better yet, would you like to sleep with my boyfriend? That usually makes you happy."

Almost involuntarily, my hand reached out and smacked her. Instantly, a handprint appeared on her cheek. Perhaps I should have felt bad, but I didn't. She was like a gnat that wouldn't go away, so I decided I'd be the fly swatter.

"You bitch," she snarled and tackled me onto the bed. I felt my hair being ripped out of my head, and then she was magically gone.

Dad grabbed her by the back of her neck and threw her across the room. It was hard to mask my smirk, but Dad didn't notice. She sat dazed against the wall while I stuffed the last of my clothes in the suitcase.

As I left, I bent down and whispered in her ear, "I know the truth."

"What truth is that?" she mumbled while rubbing her head.

"You're a bastard. You're a big fat mistake. You aren't even my whole sister." I stuck out my middle finger.

"I already know. How did you find out?"

"I've always known that you weren't really one of us." I left her huddled in the corner. "See ya' sis," I sneered while marching out the door with a mock salute. As the door shut, the sound of something shattering followed. "Too late," I shouted. "Loser."

Dad was in the car waiting for me. Mom leaned against it with a pout and a Virginia Slims cigarette dangling from her fingers. Slowly, I approached, unsure if she would scold me.

"Oh, sweetie. I wish you had told me."

"I didn't even realize until it was too late, Mom." As she stroked my hair, I rested my head on her soft breasts.

"Curly Sue, you are my everything. I'm so sorry I haven't been a better mom to you. Please believe me; I'm doing the best I can. I can scarcely make proper decisions for myself, let alone you and your sister." She lifted my chin, so we were eye to eye. "I know I'm making tons of mistakes, but remember, I would do anything for you."

"I know, Mom." And I did. My mom wasn't a terrible person. She was a person who made a lot of mistakes, but they were never intentional. To be honest, I pitied her. She was so alone. Her job was a dead end, and she was stuck raising me and the brat.

I hugged her so hard that I could feel her heart beating, hoping my love was enough to ease her guilt. The smell of her White Shoulders perfume lingered in my nostrils as a gentle reminder of her love.

Chapter 19

WE HEADED DOWN THE highway toward upstate New York. Dad listened to what he claimed was jazz, but it sounded like a bunch of instruments playing different melodies to me. I stared out the window, utterly disappointed in myself with no one to blame but me.

The letters on the building were still chipping, and the dirt road was still unpaved. We pulled up in front of the stately white building, where a nurse and two orderlies awaited my arrival.

"Dad, do I have to do this?" I moaned.

"I'm afraid you do. This time, it's going to stick. Baby, you got this." He squeezed my hand three times.

"Welcome back," said Nancy, the head nurse. She made no effort to hide her smirk.

"Thanks." I shook my head in disgust.

The friendlier of the two orderlies grabbed my bag, and the other waved for me to follow him. But before I did, I grabbed my father and hugged him as if my life depended on it.

"You go on, Sarah. You're gonna be okay. After all, you are a Brennan, and Brennan's are tough as nails."

"You bet we are." I lifted my arm to make a muscle. "Tough as nails," I repeated, and turned on my heel to take the last few steps on my own.

Nothing much had changed. The halls were still drab, with young adults roaming the corridors, wishing they were anywhere but there. I knew that look well. They were either forced to sit in on group therapy or, even worse, one-on-one where someone tried to dig into your innermost secrets. Been there, done it, bought the T-shirt, but sadly I was back again.

Room five-twenty was where I would reside for an untold amount of time. I walked in to find one single bed impeccably made and a roommate in the other. She had dark hair, which was not quite as dark as mine, more chestnut with copper streaks. Her eyeliner was thick and black, and she wore a headset connected to a Walkman.

She tried to pull the headpiece off nonchalantly, but instead, it got tangled in a mass of hair. She pulled at it. The more she did, the worse it got. "Damn it," she exclaimed in frustration at the rat's nest forming on the side of her head.

"Here, let me help." I walked over and freed her from the cord that was weaving through her hair like Medusa's serpents. "I'm Sarah."

"Thank you so much, Sarah. My attempt to be cool seems to have backfired." She chuckled in a self-deprecating way.

"No biggie. I do shit like that all the time," I assured her as I plopped down on my new bed.

"Whatcha in for?" She asked through her glossy red, cupid-like lips.

"Pain killers. I shattered my leg pretty badly, and things kind of got out of control. When I started to hallucinate, I went to my dad for help."

"Wow. That's amazing. Most kids come in kicking and screaming."

"I did that the first time. I'm an alum." I chuckled. When she cracked up too, I knew I had found a kindred spirit.

"I'm sorry. I haven't properly introduced myself. I'm Maggie Ledger from a small town that I'm sure you never heard of right outside Lake Placid, New York, and I'm addicted to coke and quaaludes."

"Quaaludes. Those are way cool."

We both were laughing again.

It didn't take long to fall back into the routine. Breakfast was at eight a.m. sharp. The buffet was similar to the one in high school. Our chosen entrée was served by some person with a glued-on smile and a hairnet. Every day, the choices were the same: pancakes or eggs, a side of fruit, and a glass of juice. Then it was off to group, where we sat around and confessed our sins. Likely the way they do in church confessionals, but I wouldn't know since we had never done that kind of thing.

After group, we got to rest from the emotional drainage. Next was lunch, followed by one-on-one therapy.

"Hi, Sarah. Come in and have a seat," she beckoned with her thick English accent from her ivory wingback chair. I took a seat on the couch across from her. On the coffee table separating us sat a yellow notepad, a ballpoint pen, a pitcher of water, and two glasses. "I'm Elaina. I am pleased to meet you."

She was a tiny bit of a thing who looked like she would make someone a lovely grandmother. Her eyes regarded me with a gentleness that other therapists had not. I crossed my fingers that she wouldn't be so bad.

"Hi, Elaina. Would you mind if I help myself to some water?" I asked, finding myself parched. I gulped the glass down and wiped my mouth with the back of my hand; my grandmother would have been appalled.

"So, Sarah. I read through your notes from your last visit with us. What brought you back here?"

That's when I knew I'd have to 'confess' in my own words and take responsibility for the addiction. Addiction therapy is extremely formulaic. I relayed the story of everything in Arizona and how happy I was until they let me go. Then, I proceeded to tell her about Star and the snake incident, the surgery, and lastly, the pills.

"This is excellent, Sarah. How do you feel when you tell me about the series of events?"

"Well, I haven't been feeling. That was part of the joy of being high." I understood what she was getting at; after all, this was not my first rodeo.

"Wonderful. I see you're willing to engage, which will make this process much easier. We need to start where you think this all began to unravel."

The clock ticked audibly as I watched the minute hand jolt every sixty seconds. When the large hand landed on the twelve and the small hand on the three, I jumped up. "Guess it will have to wait until next time. Today I get to take crochet lessons in the rec room."

"Very well, Sarah. We will delve into this a little deeper tomorrow."

"Same bat time, same bat station." I left the room, holding up a V-shape with my fingers. "Peace out."

Chapter 20

My therapy sessions were getting more complicated as Elaina probed into my life with uncomfortable questions. She was dissecting me like a piece of fruit, trying to remove the protective outer layer to get inside to the juicy stuff. The shame I was carrying with me like a heavy weight when I arrived began dissipating. I was learning forgiveness. I needed to forgive myself for not being perfect, my parents for the same reason, and Jimmy for dying.

Later that afternoon, I was lying on my bed, stomach down with my pillow over my head, and was startled by a sharp sting on my bottom. "What the fuck?" I bolted straight up. My roommate, Maggie, stood over me with a Cheshire cat grin and twinkly eyes.

"Move the tush over, lazybones," she said, shaking her behind rhythmically. I rolled over and did as she requested. She laid down next to me. We were mirror images of each other, with one arm at our side and the other behind our heads.

"Who died?" Maggie snickered sarcastically.

"My fiancé."

"Oh shit, I am so sorry. I had no idea." Her face was frozen in shock.

"Of course you didn't. Besides, I was only kidding. I mean, my fiancé died, and that is how I ended up here the first time, but that's not what's on my mind. Mags, I've been here for a month, and I want to go home. I don't want to rehash everything over and over. The past is the past. Can't I just move on?"

She rolled over on her side to face me. "I get it, Sarah. I've been here six months. Home for me is no bowl of cherries, but at least I'm not caged 24/7 by the dragon lady. On the other hand, I'm sure my mother will be on me like white on rice when I return. She is a witch, and this is my penance."

"Why are you here? You never talk about it." I pried hesitantly, unsure if she would think I was being nosey or a friend.

"I thought you'd never ask." She snickered. "In a nutshell, I fell in love, and it did not end well. I wanted to go numb, and numb was what I got."

"You don't have to answer, but what happened?" I was hoping she trusted me enough to confide in me.

"I'll tell you, but things better not change between us. Promise?"

"Promise. Cross my heart and pinky swear."

"I fell in love with a girl. She was the most exotic woman I had ever seen. Her name is Layla." Maggie's voice mellowed and took on a sing-song quality as she began to describe the love of her life. "Her hair was jet black and pin-straight, almost like Barbie's, but as dark as hair can get. Her skin, olive without a single imperfection." She practically cooed.

"Go on, go on," I insisted.

"Well, I first met her while sitting at the counter of our local diner. She stuck out like a sore thumb in our one-horse, ass-backward, whitewashed town. The old biddies whispered in the background when she entered. When I glanced up from my french fries, I felt as if I was struck by lightning. I know that sounds totally cliché, but Sarah, I'm telling you, she was pure magic. I didn't realize at the time that I was gay. I knew I wasn't attracted to boys, but that didn't make me a lesbian. Anyway, she asked if I minded if she sat next to me. I was so dumbstruck, I couldn't even reply. Later she explained to me about gaydar, which is being able to spot another gay person in a room." Maggie checked to see my reaction.

"Don't stop now," I punched her lightly on the shoulder. "I have a feeling we are getting to the juicy part."

Maggie rolled over. "One day, when my mom was at work, Layla came over. It was the first time we were going to... you know. She approached me and lightly placed her hand under my hair, upon the sensitive part of my neck. Do you know what I'm talking about?" Maggie's question was obviously rhetorical since she didn't wait for an answer. "When her dark eyes stared into mine, my knees weakened. She brought her mouth to mine. Our parted lips touched..." Maggie's voice trailed off.

"And?"

"Okay, Okay." Maggie rolled her eyes at my impatience. "Our tongues explored each other's mouths. The next thing I knew, she was leading me to my bedroom. She walked in and unbuttoned my shirt and slid down my skirt. I stood in my lace bra and panties, vulnerable and inexperienced. She removed her clothing sensuously and with intent. With one finger, she slipped down the strap of my bra and deftly removed my breast. My entire body ignited as if I was being engulfed in flames. I wasn't sure if I was scared or horny. Her teeth grazed my breast, and I moaned. That was when the seduction sped up. She freed both breasts as we tumbled to the bed. I released hers as well. I placed my mouth on her, and her back arched. Her reaction gave me the confidence to continue. Unsure of what to do next, I ran my tongue down her belly and slid off her panties. The private place between her legs was beautiful and wild. I did what came naturally. Layla guided me tenderly and was encouraging with her words and body.

"As I was on my knees, a bolt of terror tore through my body when I heard the creak of the door behind me. Within two seconds, my ears rang as my mother swatted my head. The pitch of her voice was ear-splitting. 'You sick, twisted little girl. What are you doing?'" Maggie's voice began to crack as she retold her story. "'You are going straight to hell. This is an abomination. You,' she pointed at Layla, 'Get out of my house before I call the police, you demon.' Layla grabbed her clothes and high-tailed it out of my room. That was when I understood that I was definitely gay and when I started using drugs."

"Wow. That's quite a story, Mags." Before we could continue, the door to our room burst open. The light from the hallway cast a looming nine-foot shadow.

"What the hell is going on here?" demanded Nurse Nancy, whom we lovingly, or not so lovingly, referred to as Nurse Ratchet. "We will tolerate none of that here. Do you understand?"

"None of what?" Maggie challenged with disdain.

"None of that girlie stuff. I know about you, Maggie. You keep those sick little hands to yourself."

"Nothing is going on. She's my friend."

We were both shaking our heads in disbelief.

"I don't care. Maggie, into your own bed. It's lights out."

Maggie climbed out of my bed and into her own. Nurse Ratchet shut the door.

"See. No matter how enlightened some people think we are as a society, so many people still think I'm the devil and will burn in hell."

"I don't think you're the devil at all. You, my dear friend, may be one of the strongest women I have ever met. Bravo for staying true to yourself."

Maggie's voice cut through the darkness, even in a hushed tone. "Thank you, Sarah. I'm so glad you're with me. I mean, I'm sorry about all the crappy stuff you are going through, but it's nice to have a friend I can share my secrets with."

We both stretched out our arms and clasped hands. I gave her my father's secret squeeze. One, two, three. She didn't understand what it meant, but that was okay; I did.

Chapter 21

"Come on in, Sarah," Elaina's lovely accent welcomed me.

I took my usual spot on the couch and crossed my legs in Indian style. Crisscross apple sauce, as they taught us in kindergarten. We had been going around in circles, working on breaking the code of my behavior for months, to no avail.

"How are you today?" she asked.

"Fine. Well, not exactly fine. How much longer do you think I will be here?"

Her nose crinkled a little. "Once we discover the root of the issues that are bothering you, we can begin to work toward your release." She opened my file and flipped through the pages. "It's been four months and five days. During this time, we dealt with the drugs and your need to self-medicate. All excellent and important work. Your previous therapist focused on the trauma of losing Jimmy and the resulting substance abuse. However, I believe we need to address several other issues." She must have caught my eyes rolling. "I'm not even sure you're aware of them."

"What 'issues'?" I asked, using air quotes.

"We haven't discussed your relationships with your mother or sister in depth. Not even your father. My cursory introduction to them does not give me the information we need to continue progressing."

I watched as the light played upon the pothos plant that hung in the window, wondering if a patient made her the macrame hanger that housed the plant. *I'll make one of those.*

"Sarah? Did you hear me?"

"Yes, but I'm not sure what there is to discuss."

"That's precisely it. You don't even see it. Let's start with your relationship with your sister. From what you've told me so far, your hostility seems somewhat unwarranted. Did something happen between the two of you that you haven't shared?"

I snickered. "Unwarranted? No, you're wrong. It is most definitely warranted," I barked back. "Jesus Christ!" I stood up and began pacing. The knot in my stomach had grown large enough to choke me. "Even here, she's a thorn in my side. Elaina, you have no idea what it's like to have her shadow always lingering over me." I had an overwhelming desire to stomp my feet like a three-year-old to punctuate my emotions, but the adult in me resisted.

Elaina tipped her head in a way that was similar to a dog hearing an unfamiliar noise. "Come sit back down, please," she insisted, sounding less grandmotherly than before.

Picking up the tumbler on the table, I guzzled the chilly water while deciding how to move forward. I didn't want to give a heated, guttural reaction. I wanted to sound articulate... sane.

I put the glass down and took a deep breath. "Elaina, my sister, has always gotten away with everything, and all she ever does is whine." In a lower, more ominous tone, "I can't stand the bitch."

"Tell me, what has she gotten that you have not?" she solicited without a hint of judgment.

"Where do I start? First of all, she's gorgeous. Everyone says so. They say she has a certain *Je Ne Sous Quoi*, or whatever." I made a 'W' out of my fingers. "She pisses me off how she prances around pretending not to notice everyone staring at her. Listen, it's been that way since we were little girls. Men have always fawned all over her. I remember at a Christmas party, my mom had this friend who snuck into our room and got into bed with Julie. I saw him kissing her."

Elaina's eyebrows raised in alarm.

"Oh, please. Don't look so shocked." I quipped. "It's all part of being a woman. But really, what the fuck? He wanted her and not me? That's not fair. I'm older. It should have been me," I said through tightened lips. "He should have chosen me." My voice had risen above an acceptable tone.

"Is that what you actually think? Do you believe that a woman, even little girls, should be defined by a man's sexual desires?"

"That's what I mean. It's not about sex. It's about power. Sex is power, and power is sex." I slammed my fist against the arm of the couch to punctuate the point. "Julie has all the power, and I have to fight for it. It's not fair, but at least I have Dad. The bitch doesn't even have a father."

"What does that mean?"

"Oh yeah. That's another one of those things that she's done. Right before my parents split up, the fighting got really bad. During the worst one, I overheard my mom say that Dad wasn't Julie's dad. That was possibly the worst fight ever." I had to take a moment before continuing. "I remember it vividly. I was lying in my bed with my stuffed giraffe, Gallagher. He was my best friend, and I told him everything." I remember stroking his soft fur so much that he had a bald spot on his back. "Anyway, one day Suzie Hagen, this rich bitch who sat behind me, made fun of my clothes. I was wearing a cute pink and white gingham maxi dress that my grandmother, my dad's mom, made me. In front of everyone, she was pointing and calling me Holly Hobby. I wanted to curl up in a ball and die from embarrassment. I was telling Gallagher how sad I was when I was startled by an enormous crash. I tiptoed out of my bedroom and peaked around the corner. My mom was lying on the floor with dad pinning down her shoulders.

"'What the fuck did you say?' My father bellowed.

"'I said Julie isn't yours? She is not your child. Come on, smarten up, Joe. We hadn't had sex in months.' The veins in my father's neck bulged and pulsated, but mom wouldn't stop. 'Guess what? She looks like her real father. When I look at her, I remember what a fucking loser you are.' Her voice was mocking him.

"His hands moved from her shoulder and began to squeeze her neck. Mom fought to rip his hands away. Her face was turning purple, but she couldn't pry them off. The two of them were in a tangle of contorted body parts.

"At that moment, Dad glanced up and caught me watching. I was so terrified that pee began streaming down my leg, leaving a puddle by my feet. He climbed off my mom and came to me.

"'Hi, Princess. What are you doing awake?'

"'Daddy, I peed myself.'

"'It's okay, sweetie. I'll clean it up.' He took me back to my room, helped me into a dry nightie, and tucked me into bed. 'You are my sunshine, my only sunshine. You know that, right?' And I did. The knowledge that he loved me as much as I loved him had a calming effect on me; strangely enough, he made me feel safe.

"'Yes, Daddy.' That was when we made the three-squeeze handshake we use to this day."

"That must have been terrifying for you, Sarah." The sound of Elaina's voice brought me back. It took me a moment to take in my surroundings. The familiar clock on the wall ticked. The couch was still made of crushed velvet, and the light danced upon the pathos plant.

"It was"—my forehead squinched up—"but I haven't given it much thought over the years."

"That is exactly why we need to keep talking. Can you see that?"

She was right. I had so much more work to do. Although I thought my time in Arizona was my becoming an adult, I was wrong. This would be my baptism into adulthood.

Chapter 22

WHEN I RETURNED TO my room, I found Maggie with the headset of her Walkman pressed against her ears. She was jamming hard on her air guitar. Her eyes were closed, and she was wearing my silver and black banana clip.

"All we need is music. Sweet, sweet, sweet, sweet, sweet, music." I gleaned from the lyrics she was listening to her favorite cassette, Van Halen's Diver Down. She listened to it night and day. Her singing was loud and horrendously out of tune. Seeing her unabashedly letting go was exactly what I needed after my exhausting session.

"Hey," I yelled from across the room, but she didn't answer. "Mags," I called a little louder. Still no response. I grabbed my pillow and hit her over the head.

"What the fuck?" she whooped. "Not funny." She grabbed her pillow and hit me across the face. We broke out into an old-fashioned pillow fight. The kind Julie and I had when we were little.

"Stop. Stop. I surrender." I dropped my pillow and held up both hands. My cheeks ached from smiling. "No more."

We both plopped down on my bed, out of breath. "How was your one-on-one today?" Maggie asked.

"Brutal. I can't talk about it anymore. I'm sorry, I'm frigging spent. Hearing you sing was exactly what I needed. Thank you." I rolled with laughter.

"Anytime. I'm at your disposal to mock and ridicule." She winked.

"No, really. I don't think I'd make it through this without you." Grabbing her hand, I squeezed it three times. "I love you."

She turned to me. Our eyes lingered on each other more than what seemed normal.

I broke our gaze first. "Dinner time. Let's go scarf down some chow."

"Great. I'm starving. Help me up."

I grabbed her hand, and off we went.

Life in rehab continued much the same way. Day by day, Elaina painfully helped me realize I was taking my anger out on Julie. I either didn't want to or couldn't see that the ones I loved most were doing the most damage. The real people I was mad at were my parents. Julie was merely the lighting rod I had inadvertently chosen to receive my wrath. She wasn't to blame for Mom cheating and getting pregnant, and she might have been more traumatized than I. After all, how would I have reacted if it was me that got that earth-shattering news?

As far as my jealousy of her beauty, I was still jealous, but I concluded beauty was not always a blessing. Sometimes there was a heavy price to pay.

Man, I was so much more messed up than I ever imagined. I thought I was normal—whatever that meant—and somewhat well-adjusted outside of the drug-seeking behavior. I knew I had to make things right with my sister.

I sat in the tiny phone booth and tapped in our phone number. With each ring, I drummed my fingers a little faster on the small table under the phone. I had planned what I was going to say, but my mind went blank as soon as the ringing stopped.

"Hey, Sis." I tried to sound casual. The telephone cord took the brunt of my anxiety as I twisted it into various shapes.

"Hey, Sarah. How are you?" The timber of her voice told me she wasn't still mad.

"I'm doing okay. Really." I forced a smile, as if she could see through the receiver. "Julie, I'm so sorry." My voice was shaking.

"About what?"

"I have been such a bitch to you, and I said some really horrible things before I left."

"Sarah, it takes two to tango. Instead of being supportive, I went on the attack. Oh god, that was horrible. I think it was the worst fight we ever had."

We both laughed at the craziness. "I'm sorry," we blurted out simultaneously.

"I promise I will do better, Jul. You've always had my back, and I want you to know that I really appreciate it."

"Life hasn't always been easy for us. We're all a little fucked up, but you can always count on me. Pinky swear."

"Pinky swear," I responded. "Let's both try to do better. As Mom always told us, we are all we have. God, I wish I could give you a giant hug right now. Will you come to visit on the next family day?"

"Of course. I've been waiting for you to ask. You sound good."

"I think I am. I've got to fly. It's time for lights out. I love you."

"I love you too."

Chapter 23

FALL TURNED TO WINTER, and with it came inches of powdered snow that made everything it touched feel like it came out of a fairytale. Maggie and I walked around the property bundled in our winter coats, hats, scarves, and mittens. Everything except the coats matched because we knitted them together in art therapy. After my lungs brought in the coldness, a smokey puff would be released a second later.

"Maggie, I think I might be a terrible person." I shivered, more from my realization than the cold.

"Don't be ridiculous. You're amazing."

"No, really. For as long as I can remember, I have treated my sister like shit. I've blamed her for everything. What the fuck is wrong with me?"

Maggie stopped dead in her tracks and moved my face to ensure I was looking directly at her. "You need to stop punishing yourself. You were a kid, and kids only learn from what they see. Monkey see monkey do, and all that. You're a grownup now, and you're making amends. That is being an actual adult." She wiped the snow from my eyelashes. There it was again. That sensation I had that night we were on my bed. We stayed that way until another resident passed by and threw a snowball in our direction.

"Hey, you chuckleheads, snowball fight out front. Let's go get Nurse Ratchet," called Lexi, another long-time narco user.

We dashed to the open field and packed the fresh powder into frozen spherical ammunition. We hid behind a giant old oak tree, protecting ourselves from incoming fire. Our fingers and toes went numb as we roared with laughter and screamed for hours.

When we returned inside, we huddled around a hot radiator cover as we sipped hot chocolate. I imagined it's what kids felt when having a normal childhood. How was rehab becoming more comfortable than my actual home, and the residents more like family?

Nighttime rolled around, and my body was as limp as an overcooked noodle. I craved the comfort of my bed. After a long, hot shower, I crawled deep into my sheets, still shivering from the day's events. As I drifted off, Maggie tiptoed in.

"Hey," I whispered.

"Hi, sorry to wake you."

"You didn't. Are you coming to bed?"

"Yeah." A moment passed by. "Sarah?"

I propped myself up on my elbow to give her my full attention. She sat down on the end of my bed. "What's going on, Mags? Why are you so sad?"

"That phone call I got at dinner was from my mom. She's coming to pick me up tomorrow." She cried into her hands. "This may sound fucked up, but I don't want to leave. Sarah, she'll never accept me. She honestly believes she can pray away my being gay." It was the first time I saw her shed a tear my whole time there. She was the one who gave others pep talks and was the shoulder we all leaned on.

"Oh shit. Somehow, I didn't think this day would come. I imagined we would be released at the same time." I got out of bed and plopped down next to her, placing my arm around her shoulder. She leaned in and cried even harder.

"Okay, fuck this." She wiped the wetness from her eyes. "This is not how I'm going out. I refuse to let this be how you remember me; a bleary-eyed, snotty-nose mess. I'm going to hit the shower, and then you and I will have a dance party. Are you in?" Her eyes lit up.

"Hell yeah, I'm in. Diver Down?"

"Damn straight. All the way down." And she danced her way into the bathroom.

While she showered, I understood that I, too, was running out of time. This was not my home and the people, not my family. I would have to return to reality as well, but not before I did one more thing.

Maggie walked out of the bathroom wearing a gargantuan pair of sweatpants that swam on her tiny frame and a crop top. Her hair was still dripping wet with water, slowly saturating her shirt.

She clicked open her Walkman, removed her favorite cassette, and slid it into my boombox. "Let's get this party started," she announced with all the enthusiasm of a kid going to a house party. She took my hand, bringing me to my feet, and hit play. Pretty Woman came blaring out of the speakers, and we were off. We spun around the room, flailing our arms, and moving with the rhythm. We were young, wild, and almost free.

After the first side of the tape ran its course, we collapsed on the floor.

"Boy, did I need that," Maggie panted.

I crawled over to her, snuggling up close, placing my hand on her firm, flat belly, and my head on her chest. I felt each inhale and the beating of her heart still thumping with exhaustion. She spun my hair between her fingers with one hand and ran her other hand down my spine. My heart began to race, but not from the dancing.

The uncertainty petrified me. She tipped her body enough to make me readjust my position, and when I did, she put her lips tenderly upon mine. With the meeting of our lips, my hairs tingled as they came to attention. I melted into her. As we rearranged into a new position, she took the lead and hovered over me with her knees on either side of my thighs. Her wet hair fell forward, leaving us in a damp tunnel.

I hovered my hand over her breast, where her nipples remained erect from her wet T-shirt. "May I?" My chest was heaving in anticipation.

"Sarah, I have wanted you for so long, but didn't want to ruin our friendship. You're too important to me. If this is going to make things weird, maybe we shouldn't," her words said, but her body was telegraphing a completely different message.

"You aren't losing me. On the contrary, you've found me." With that, she kissed me deeper, pulling off her shirt and exposing two alabaster, flawless breasts that were smooth and creamy to the touch. I cupped each one in my hands. Touching her made my body ache. She responded by throwing her head back and arching. I touched her the way I liked to be touched, hoping she would respond. She stood and removed her sweatpants, revealing her nudity. Her pubic area was bare, which I found titillating.

"Do you want me to undress you, or are you more comfortable doing it yourself?" Maggie asked, appreciating I was a novice in this area.

"You do it." My fingers were trembling. She delicately removed my shirt and kissed my neck. Using her foot, she pushed down my shorts and panties. As the shorts slid down my legs, so did she.

I gasped as she explored my nether region.

"I've been dying to know how you taste. You remind me of smokey butterscotch, and I love smokey butterscotch." She stood and led me to the bed. "This is so much better. It will be easier to devour you." She wrapped her arms around my legs, dropping my knees to both sides.

When I was about to orgasm, I raised my pelvis to meet her. I caught a glimpse of her eyes watching me, which sent me over the edge. I had to cover my mouth to muffle my moans of pleasure.

"How did you like that?" she enquired with a devilish smirk.

"Oh my god. If that is what being a lesbian is like, sign me up." I gave her two thumbs up and a cheesy smile.

"Sarah, that didn't make you a lesbian. I am one, so I know what I'm talking about. I have zero interest in men. Zero desire to kiss them, fuck them, or have any physical relationship, and from what you told me, you do."

"So, what does that make me?" I was confused.

"It makes you fricking lucky. You now have the entire population to choose from. Listen, you don't have to label yourself. It's society that wants us all to conform to some stupid Stepford wife conventionality. You are now free, my lovely Sarah." Then she kissed me, and we started over again.

Saying goodbye to my best friend and now lover was terribly painful. I waved as she was driving off with her mother and aunt. She sat in the backseat with her hand pressed against the rear window, and her sad eyes were overflowing with tears. She appeared more like a prisoner in that car than she ever did in rehab.

Chapter 24

When spring came, the snow melted, and tiny crocuses peeked their colorful heads out. I knelt and investigated their soft purple leaves. "Well, hello, little one," I addressed the tiny life fighting its way into the sunshine. "I think it's time we both bloom and take our place in the world."

I strolled back to the building, arriving in the nick of time for my session with Elaina.

"Come on in," she called from somewhere inside in response to my knocking. "Hi, Sarah. You look frozen. Your nose is all red." She giggled. "Come have a seat and put the throw over you."

"Thanks." I did as she had suggested and pulled the navy afghan up to my chin, letting out a little shiver.

"How are you today?"

"I think I'm starting to understand, Elaina. At least abstractly." The revelations were slowly coming to light, so I tried to find the words that matched. "I don't really know who I am. Me, Sarah Brennan. I always viewed myself as an extension of my mom. I believed I should think, dress, and behave like her." My lower lip started to quiver. "Oh, Elaina. I want to start all over."

Elaina nodded in approval. "Congratulations, Sarah. You're on your way. The journey of self-discovery doesn't end with this epiphany. This is the beginning of your story. You are ready for your do-over."

"Are you saying what I think you're saying?" I asked incredulously.

"I believe so. I am saying it's time to go home. You are ready to build a life. You'll have to follow ground rules. I highly recommend continuing therapy, as there is so much more that needs to be unearthed. Still, I am confident that drugs will not be part of your future journey."

Tears inched their way down my cheeks.

After our session, I waited in line to use the payphone. There were two people ahead of me, and I couldn't wait. I begged Annette, a girl who lived two doors down, to let me go before her. She agreed once I promised to give her my dessert every night until I left.

"Hello," Mom answered.

"Hey, Mom. Can Julie pick up the extension? I have something to tell you both."

Mom yelled Julie's name as if she were a mile away instead of in the next room. I chuckled; some things never changed.

"Hello," Julie's high-pitched voice joined the conversation.

"Hey, Squirt. Are you both on?"

"We're here," their voices sang in unison.

"Guess who is being sprung on account of good behavior?"

All three of us squawked in glee. The Brennan Girls were going to be back together.

That weekend I stood by the entrance, or in that case, the exit, and waited to be called. I felt a gentle tap on my shoulder, and when I turned around, my shrink was smiling at me.

"I couldn't very well let my favorite patient leave without saying goodbye." Elaina slipped a piece of paper into my hand. "This is my home number. If you tell anyone I gave it to you, I will deny it. Call anytime, day or night, and I promise I'll pick up."

I hugged her tightly. "Thank you doesn't seem adequate."

"Sarah, there are a couple of people waiting outside for you." Nurse Ratchet smiled more pleasantly than I had ever seen her. Which made me wonder, was it she who changed or I?

"Coming." I opened the door, and Mom and Julie were waiting to greet me with their arms wide open. This may have been my second departure, but I was sure it would be my last. The three of us hugged and kissed until we almost toppled over. We climbed into our beat-up sedan, and the tires kicked up brown, smokey dirt as we left. I had no reason to look back.

Mom quizzed me about all the goings-on at rehab. I kept my stories of self-discovery brief and only shared the light-hearted adventures of Maggie and me. I assured her I was ready to face life sober.

"Well, that's a bummer," scoffed Mom. "You can drink. It was drugs you had the issue with."

"No, Mom. No more drugs or drinking. I'm done." My body tightened, knowing she was never going to understand.

"Listen, sweetie. I get they told you not to drink, but that's the doctors covering their asses. You only need to stay away from the hard stuff." She droned on, but I tuned her out. Instead, I stared out at the farmland passing by my window, wishing I could jump out of the car.

Chapter 25

I SLEPT FOR DAYS after returning home. I think the past year caught up to me all at once. When I was ready to confront the future, I understood that I needed to leave Westfield. As much as I loved Mom and Julie, it would be counterproductive to stay, but where would I go? I opened my checkbook and stared at the balance. My bank account had $2,843 left from my job at the ranch.

I spent several afternoons at the library searching for travel destinations. I read issues of Frommer's Travel Guides from front to back and flipped through dozens of issues of Travel & Leisure magazine. I diligently took notes of places to go and where to stay. The photographs of mountains and beaches were mesmerizing, but I found the one place that called to me. I immediately fell in love with the breathtaking beaches and the white stone houses that speckled the island of Crete.

Mom was in her usual place, with the latest Jackie Collins novel in one hand and a scotch in the other. I sat in the chair across from her and pulled out all my research. The last piece of paper showed a carefully outlined itinerary.

"Sarah, honey, I'm not so sure about this. Besides, I don't think you even have enough money to pull it off. I think you should call your father."

I reached over her head, pulled the phone off the cradle, and dialed. I explained my plan to him, thinking he would be supportive.

He also tried to dissuade me by bringing up my past failures, but they both needed to be reminded of my successes. "Dad, I've got this. I am not a little girl, and I am anything but fragile. I basically lived in Arizona on my own and was fine. If it hadn't been for the accident, I would have stayed there," I reasoned. "I'm a big girl. I will find a way to do this with or without your blessing."

He sighed in defeat, making me promise up and down that I would be careful.

"Daddy, one last question. Can I have some money? I think I may need a little more than what I have saved." I held my breath, awaiting his response. He begrudgingly agreed. I was getting the hell out of Jersey.

Mom and I called the airlines and booked me on a flight leaving June 15th from JFK airport in New York. I packed everything I owned, which was a huge mistake. One that I would regret later in the week. The day before my departure, all the news stations were taken over by the story of a hijacking out of Athens airport. A terrorist group commandeered the plane and threatened to kill the passengers with Jewish-sounding names.

Mom and I sat glued to the television, unsure what to do.

"Mom, should we cancel?" I was beginning to panic.

"Actually, this is most likely the safest time to fly. I'm sure the police and guards will be everywhere," she countered, assuring me that I would be okay.

I never gave my Jewish heritage a moment's thought because I was raised Christian. "Mom, will they be able to tell my grandmother is Jewish by looking at me? If they find out, will they kill me?" I was getting scared.

"No, baby. I'll go downtown to Bower's pharmacy and buy you a crucifix. We will put you in a dress and your hair in a bun. You'll look like a nun in training. Ingenious, huh?"

"If you think so," I answered sheepishly.

The next morning, we drove to the airport; as I exited, she took my hand. "Whatever you do, do not stay in Athens airport. Make your connection and get out. Do you understand?"

"Yes, Mom." I hoisted my suitcase out of the trunk and set it on its wheels. Grabbing the strap, I pulled it behind me, waving as I went.

The counter for the airline was decked out in red and blue. I handed the paper ticket to the woman behind the counter. When she opened it up, she informed me the plane would be leaving momentarily. I checked my watch, realizing it had stopped several hours before.

"What? Oh no. I can't miss it. What should I do?" I demanded.

"Here, give me your bag. If you run, you may be able to board before the cabin door closes. Go now," she said when I hesitated.

I handed over my suitcase and dashed for the gate. I pushed past hordes of people milling about, speeding through security and up the jetway. "Hold the door," I shouted, squeezing in as it was about to close. On the way to my seat, I glanced around the empty aircraft. Unease settled into my chest.

The flight was painfully long, and I was warned that I needed to always stay on high alert. The terror wracking my body had me longing for a glass of wine to calm my nerves. Instead, I bit my nails until reaching the pink skin underneath. After over eleven hours in the air, we touched down. I bowed my head in silent prayer, thanking God for our safe arrival.

We deplaned, and I followed the tiny crowd, hoping to find the luggage collection area. As we maneuvered through the unfamiliar airport, I spotted soldiers with machine guns slung over their arms. The signage was in a language I didn't understand, and the voices expelled words that had no meaning to me. As I tried to familiarize myself with the area, I lost sight of the other passengers. "Excuse me, can you tell me where I can find the luggage carousel?" I asked a soldier carrying a sizeable rifle. He shrugged, indicating he didn't understand what I was saying.

I did my best to pantomime what I was trying to get across. He finally caught on and motioned for me to follow. At last, we found the carrousel with the luggage from my flight. The friendly soldier tipped his hat and disappeared into the distance.

My suitcase was ejected through a hole in the wall, landing on the conveyor belt that would send it my way. As it passed, I stuck out my hand to grab it, but because of the weight, it dragged me several feet before I lost my grip and fell to the floor. I had to wait for it to come around again. When it did, I was prepared. I took a stance like a baseball player coming up to bat. I rubbed my hands on my dress, removing any moisture, but before I had a chance, a hand skimmed my side and plucked it from the conveyor belt.

I followed the hand to see to whom it belonged. He had to be over six feet tall, well-tanned, and wore gold-rimmed Giorgio Armani sunglasses. His charcoal suit and light blue and white striped tie were meticulously pressed, which only made me more aware of how disheveled I must have looked.

"Thank you so much. I think I over-packed," I said with a hint of a smile.

"Paracaló," his deep voice replied.

"I'm sorry, I don't speak Greek," I chirped in embarrassment.

"That's okay. My English is fairly good. My name is Stavros." His eyes twinkled in a way that made me feel as if I knew him already.

"Hey, Stavros. I'm Sarah." I extended my hand to shake his, which he turned over, and kissed the back of it softly, boosting my interest to another level.

"I am so happy we ran into each other; no pun intended. I'm catching a connecting flight to Crete, but I have no idea where to go." My surroundings were so foreign, it was overwhelming as I scanned around. "I promised my mother I wouldn't hang around the airport longer than necessary. By any chance, would you know where I need to go?" I used my sexiest voice while nibbling on the side of my finger.

"As it so happens, I am heading there as well. Let me show you the way."

"Thank you." I grabbed the strap of my suitcase and pulled it along, but with every few steps, it tumbled over.

"Sarah, allow me." He took the handle and glided it across the airport floor.

I followed him out of the building to a smaller terminal a few hundred yards away. It was an entirely different experience from the international airport. This airport was small and dimly lit. Chickens ran around uncaged, families yelled to one another, and people ate meats wrapped in bread.

Once at the gate, he took my ticket and spoke to the attendant. When he returned, he informed me we would sit together on the plane, and he'd give me the lay of the land, so to speak.

"Thank you so much for everything. You've been a real lifesaver."

His eyes twinkled with the flattery. As he ran his hand through his hair, the sleeve of his shirt raised, exposing an incredible timepiece.

"That's a beautiful watch," I said, hoping I wasn't too forward.

"Thank you." He held out his wrist for us both to admire. "I get excellent deals in my line of business."

That piqued my interest. "What do you do?"

"I import and export fine jewelry and gemstones. Trust me; it's not as glamourous as it sounds." He kept his tone nonchalant. "When I was a young boy growing up on Crete, all the tourists flocked into Chania to buy out the jewelry stores. The gold that Greece and Italy produce is of an exceptionally high caliber. When this gold is manipulated by our artisans and combined with a precious stone, it is magnificent. I would be happy to show you." His accent was sultry.

"I would love that," I exclaimed. Probably too quickly.

We boarded the small puddle jumper plane that held only twenty passengers. As we traveled, he explained that Crete is where he maintains a vacation home, but his home base is in Athens. He travels all over the world for weeks at a time. He regaled me with stories as we passed over the crystal blue water. The landscape was dotted with white buildings on the approach, exactly as the books had described.

"Where are you staying?" Stavros probed.

"I have a reservation at a youth hostel in Chania."

"You will love it. Crete is unlike anywhere else in the world."

"Will you be in Chania as well?"

"Ah, no. I have a small villa in the mountains, near my childhood home. I don't come into the city too often. Tourists." His nose was turned up in disdain. "I hope I do not offend."

"No offense taken," I assured him.

"If you would be interested, I would be delighted to show you around this evening. Show you the hot spots and where the jewelry stores are located."

I glanced down and saw my dress had gross stains on the front. I used my fingers to tuck in some of the loose hair, trying to make myself more presentable. I gave up, realizing I was way past the point of trying to pull off cute.

"Does your silence and rosy cheeks mean yes or no? I am not familiar with this reaction."

"That sounds wonderful, but can we do it another day? I am in desperate need of clean clothes and sleep."

"Naï."

"I'm sorry. I don't speak a word of Greek."

I read the amusement in his eyes. "Naï means 'yes' in Greek. Yes, I would love to take you another day. Perhaps tomorrow?"

"Naï." Head tilt, hair strand, crooked smile.

Chapter 26

DUE TO THE TURMOIL in the world, most of the hostel rooms were empty, allowing me to have a room of my own. It was sparsely furnished with two sets of bunk beds, a small end table, and a rickety dresser, not unlike my room in rehab. A shared unisex bathroom with several toilets and showers was at the end of a long, dimly lit hallway.

The jets from the cold shower cooled my body to a bearable temperature. On return to my room, I switched the ceiling fan to high and fell into a deep sleep. I awoke eighteen hours later to a knocking on my door. Groggily, I shuffled over, rubbing the sleep out of my eyes. Upon opening the door, I found Stavros standing in the hall wearing khaki shorts and a white T-shirt. His bicep was inked with a yin-yang tattoo that peeked out of his tight, short sleeve.

"I'm sorry. Did we have plans?" I was still confused from the time change.

"Naï ... I mean, yes. It is tomorrow. Is it not?"

I noted the time on the clock. "Uh, yeah, I guess it is. Would you mind waiting in the lobby? I need ten minutes to pull myself together." Before he walked away, I called out, "Wait, what should I wear?"

He flashed me a brilliant smile. "Bring your swimsuit. I'm taking you on an adventure."

I threw my bathing suit, towel, and sunscreen into a bag and locked my door. I stopped in the bathroom for a quick sprucing. I fluffed my hair, adjusted my T-shirt, exposing one shoulder ala Flashdance, and set off to the lobby to meet my tour guide.

We hopped in his little red Alpha Romeo convertible and set out on the day's exploration. Stavros drove at an alarming speed, taking hairpin turns, hugging the mountain, and leaving me on edge. He veered off what I would call a country lane and into the parking lot of a small shack-like structure. From the outside, I spotted skinned rabbits hanging in the window by their back legs and fish laying on beds of ice. An old "Open" sign flailed loosely in the doorway.

Stavros came around and opened my door. He stuck out his hand to help me out of the car. I felt a little giddy, like I was in an old Grace Kelly movie, and he was playing the leading man.

"Welcome to my cousin Nicholas' restaurant. I have something very exciting planned."

"Yasou, 'ti kanis," yelled a young man as he approached.

"Ah, here he is, my cousin Nick."

The two men hugged as they patted each other on the back hardily and released with a kiss on each cheek. The cousins spoke speedily in their native tongue. There was lots of nodding and glances my way.

"Let's all suit up, shall we? Nicky will show you where you can change." Stavros handed me my beach bag.

I followed his cousin to a back room in the restaurant with crates of dried fruit and stacks of cans. "What the fuck am I doing?" I muttered. *When in Rome, or in this case, Greece.* I changed out of my street clothes and into my new emerald green bikini with a matching sarong.

When I returned, Stavros was sitting at a table reading a newspaper.

He glanced up as I approached. His eyes grew larger, and a half-smile crossed his face. "Wow. I hope you don't find this too forward, but you are simply stunning."

"Not at all. I'm flattered." I gave a three-sixty view and ended with a little curtsy.

We jumped into a four-wheel-drive truck and went back down the mountain. An old wooden dock with small fishing boats lined the rocky shore. It was reminiscent of a painting I once saw my sister do.

"What's the name of the boat?" I wanted to know since I was unfamiliar with the Greek alphabet. The two men smirked, apparently sharing a private joke.

"The Naughty Lady," Stavros replied with a devilish grin.

We climbed aboard the small vessel. The engine started with a quick pull, and we were off. After ten minutes, Nicholas set anchor.

Stavros put his arm around me and pointed to several blurry things that sat at the bottom of the crystal blue water. "Do you see those small round crustaceans?"

"Yes, what are they?" I was fascinated.

"Sea urchin. They are a delicacy and will be served tonight at the restaurant. Are you a good swimmer?"

"I can hold my own," I retorted with a certain cockiness.

"Then in you go. We will free dive. That means you will have a mask and snorkel, but you must hold your breath as you go down and then blow out all the water on your return up top. Does that make sense?"

No, it did not. My only swimming experience was in my grandparent's pool, but I played it cool. "Of course, it makes sense. I can't wait to begin."

I was about to jump in when he stopped me.

"Hold on a minute. The urchin has sharp spines. You will need these to pick them up." He handed me thick black rubber gloves.

"Nick isn't wearing any?" I noted.

"No, but he's been doing this his whole life. His hands are calloused from years of gathering urchin."

"I'm good." I held my hands together and dove off the back of the boat into the crystal blue Aegean Sea. When I came up for air, the two sleek tanned gods were in the water with me.

"Pame," Nick called out and dove deep. He plucked the urchins from their resting place and piled them into a net he had slung around his body.

"Would you like to try?" Stavros asked me.

"On second thought, I think I'll watch from here," I said, when I saw how far down they were going.

"I think that is a wise idea. We will be right back." He slipped below the surface and was gone, gliding through the water like a mythical sea creature. Both Nick and Stavros circled each other, communicating with hand signals. It played out like some kind of underwater dance.

I held onto the boat ladder while it rode the current. *This is so crazy*, I thought, still stunned by the absurdity of it all. This would blow Mom's mind. I watched them dive, return for air, and then go down again for at least an hour. They never ran out of breath.

After several more dives, we returned to shore. They quickly sorted through their treasure, sending the smaller ones back into the sea and keeping the mature ones. On our drive back to the restaurant, the men roared with laughter. I didn't know what we were joking about, but I joined in, nonetheless.

We sat at a simple wooden table with four chairs. The men covered it with newspaper and poured out their delicacies. Nick pulled out a small knife and cut around the edges of the crustation, then pulled off the top. Inside were tiny, vibrant orange seeds clinging to the inside of the dome. With a spoon, he hollowed some out and passed it to me while mouthing the motion to eat. The brininess was not overpowering like some seafood, and a subtle sweetness followed. I rubbed my belly and rolled my eyes to demonstrate that I loved them.

A waiter brought a bottle of clear liquid over, along with three glasses.

"What is it?" I asked anyone who would answer. Nick smiled and encouraged me to drink.

"It is called raki. It's Greek moonshine, so to speak. Take it easy. It will, as they say, knock your socks off," Stavros warned.

Shit, what do I do? My internal struggle lasted for only moments before I tossed back the firewater. We drank several shots as Nick zipped a harmonica across his lips, playing songs from his childhood. I stood to use the restroom but couldn't find my balance. Before tipping over, Nick grabbed me.

"I told you to be careful," Stavros chastised. "I better take her home," he told Nick, while gathering me in his arms.

There was no denying I was drunk, because my words came out in a garble of consonants as my head bobbed on my neck like an unstrung marionette.

"I'm so sorry," I slurred and patted both men on the side of their faces.

"Daxi," said Nick. "Daxi."

I woke up some hours later in an incredibly soft yet unfamiliar bed. Swinging my legs over the side, I rose to stand up, but my head spun as I did so. Bile lurched up into my throat, threatening to spill out.

"Woah, not so fast." Stavros came forward and sat me back down on the bed. "I told you to take it easy. Raki is not for the faint of heart."

"Lesson learned," I muttered while trying to restrain my body from ejecting any sort of unwanted fluids.

"I will bring you something to eat. It is an old Greek cure for a hangover."

Laying back on the bed, I tried to put together the pieces of the evening. I remembered drinking a few shots of some hellish liquor and eating the sea urchin. Everything got foggy after that. I hoped I didn't do anything too embarrassing.

Why didn't he take me back to the hostel? I supposed it was possible he was a decent guy who wanted to make sure I was okay. Yeah, that's the story I decided to go with.

A short while later, Stavros returned with a bowl of piping hot soup on a tray.

"That smells yummy. What is it?"

"It's called patsas. It will fix you up in a jiffy."

I lapped up the broth but found the chicken hard to chew.

Stavros tried to hide his smile as I struggled to swallow it. "Tasty, right?" He nodded.

"Yeah, but is this chicken? I'm having trouble with the texture."

"It's not chicken. It's tripe and pig's feet," he revealed casually, as if he was saying it was bacon and eggs.

Beige liquid from the deepest recess of my intestines splattered all over the floor and white bed cover. So much for not doing anything embarrassing.

Chapter 27

STAVROS LET ME LEAN on him as he guided me to the bathroom. I stood under the multi-stream shower heads, allowing the water to pulsate the cobwebs from my brain and eradicate the vomit vapers from my nose. When I stepped out of the steam, I found a sundress hanging on the back of the door. I slipped it on, and the satin glided down my body as if it was made for me.

I returned to the bedroom, expecting to see Stavros, but the room was empty. I strolled the halls, trying to find my host. Enormous windows graced each room like picture frames for the azure sea.

I found him sitting outside on the telephone. He held his hand up to tell me to wait a moment. I sat down on the empty chaise next to him.

His voice was raised, and he gibbered rapidly. "Bastardo," he muttered after slamming the phone down. I didn't have to speak Greek to understand what that word meant. After a beat or two, the angry aura surrounding him evaporated, leaving only his suave persona.

"How are you feeling? You less piqued, as they say."

"I can't thank you enough for your kindness. The whole drinking and vomiting thing was so embarrassing. I'm so sorry." I forced a smile. "It's probably time for me to go back to the hostel. Would you mind giving me a ride?"

He let out a long sigh. "I have a better idea. As you may have heard, I have a deal that is about to go sour and need to return to Athens until I can get it settled. Why don't we retrieve your things from the hostel, and you can stay here?" He put up an authoritative hand to keep me from talking. "Before you say no, please take into consideration that I will not be here. I will stay in my Athens apartment for at least a week, possibly two or three. The run of the house will be yours. I promise it is much safer and more comfortable than that small, dank room."

"But you don't even know me. I might be a thief, rip you off, or be a con artist and suck you dry." *Ugh*, I thought to myself in embarrassment when I realized how it sounded. He had trouble hiding his smirk. "I mean, steal all your money," I tried to clarify.

"Don't worry about me. I am an excellent judge of character. If I were not, my business would have folded long ago. When dealing with wholesalers and jewelers, I would be doomed if I couldn't tell a fake from the real thing. That goes for both jewelry and people."

A few hours later, the bleak hostel room was empty, and my personal effects were stowed away in a sunny white concrete villa, exactly like the ones in the travel magazines. I could hardly believe my good luck.

Later that evening, we dined on a beautiful feast of fresh flakey fish from the sea and ripe cucumber with tzatziki. The garlic was so potent it oozed out of my pores. We sipped on small glasses of grappa, raki's less dangerous cousin. Over several hours, he shared his world and childhood with me. Growing up poor, his life's ambition was to prove to his peers that he was more than his past. He wanted to show the world that he no longer wore ill-fitting clothes and shoes with holes in the soles. Letting me in the way he did allowed me to share pieces of myself that I would have ordinarily kept hidden. His eyes were that of a victorious gladiator, not innocent prey.

When the sun came up, Stavros was no longer a stranger. I rose from my chair to go get some sleep. As I was leaving, he took my hand and kissed it. "Eisai o agapinenos mou."

"What does that mean?"

"I will tell you when I return. Please make yourself at home. Nothing is off limits, and the housekeeper and groundskeeper can help you with anything you may need."

"Thank you, and safe travels. I'll see you in a week or two."

He kissed my hand.

Once I was alone in the bedroom, I dropped to my knees. *Oh my god! I cannot believe this is happening.* I was stifling my laughter so no one would overhear.

Once the giggles subsided, I wondered how everything was going to play out when he got back. Would he want something from me in return for staying in his villa? I had nothing to offer, except the obvious. I was grateful to have some time to mull over the implications of my new living situation.

By the time I awoke, it was afternoon, and I had the house to myself. I stood on the balcony watching the boats glide in a technicolor parade in and out of the harbor. I literally pinched myself to make sure it wasn't a dream. It would have been a great place for Julie to set up her easel.

Moments later, I rambled off to find some coffee and a telephone. I found both in the kitchen. Picking up the receiver, I made the first of three calls.

"Daddy?"

"Well, hot damn! If it's not the world traveler. How are you, darling?"

I gave him a synopsis of the trip, the soldiers at the airport, and a description of my room at the hostel. I intentionally omitted all the details that led me to live in a Greek villa. After hanging up, I had the same conversation with my mother and Julie.

The last phone call would be the hardest to make. I hesitated before dialing.

"Hello."

"Hi," I screeched, unable to hide my joy.

"Sarah! Oh my god. Where have you been? I thought you forgot about me!"

Hearing her voice was like taking in a breath of fresh air. "Maggie, I could never forget about you."

She may have been my lover for one night, but she had become a part of me.

We chatted for several minutes, catching up on the latest happenings. She was not surprised I was involved with another man or landed in a storybook villa. Unfortunately, her story was not as dreamy and adventurous as mine. Maggie's mother hadn't changed her archaic way of thinking. In her eyes, Maggie was still a sinner who would be punished until she changed her ways. Without any money or friends, she had no escape.

My chest was heavy with empathy as she relayed her saga. I wished with everything I was that I could do something for her. In many ways, I was as helpless as she was. We said our goodbyes, wished each other well, and hung up. Tears trickled down my cheeks, but I swiped them away.

Enough of that, I told myself, leaving Maggie and my feelings in the past. I threw on my bathing suit and walked down the steep stone steps to the beach, where Stavros had a private pavilion. I lounged under the navy and white tent, sipping cold peach nectar.

In a short time, my alabaster skin turned a hazelnut brown. One day melded into the next with no thought of anything but the here and now and which caftan to throw over my ever-expanding array of bikinis.

I no longer behaved like a guest and began to take my privilege for granted by bathing nude on the terrace on the housekeeper's day off. I stretched out on the mesh chaise, enjoying the sun lapping at my body. The sound of footsteps came from nowhere. I threw the towel next to me over my naked body.

"Umm, I'm so sorry. I didn't know you were coming back today," I stuttered, seeing Stavros standing at the doorway.

His chest heaved with laughter. "Do not be so conservative on my account. European women sunbathe nude all the time. It is only Americans who are embarrassed by the human body." He walked over, unpeeled my arms away from my chest, and tossed the towel back over the chair. "Ah, yes, that is better. I hope you are not offended, but you have lovely breasts."

"This is all so foreign to me." I saw his eyes drinking me in. "I've never done this before."

His entire body radiated with desire. I have seen the same glazed-over look in dozens of men's eyes. As he moved closer, I could practically taste the cherries he had been eating. He leaned down over me; the proximity of his lips made me crave their touch. He parted his lips, and I responded in kind. Our tongues mingled, making us both tremble. My back arched, and my legs fell slightly open, allowing him to slip his fingers inside and explore my wetness.

"I see you like that." He sighed softly, letting his warm breath play on my neck. He continued his manipulation as I moved in response. It wasn't long before I succumbed to the pleasure he gifted me.

"Come stay with me in my bedroom. There is no need for separate lodging. I want to make you cum always, and I will, with you in my bed."

I moved from the guest room into his bed, where we explored each other's bodies in detail.

When Stavros was in town, he would take me on long drives, showing me where he grew up, had his first kiss, and made his first business deal. Our evenings were consumed with lovemaking. Stavros was a bit of an artist, often starting at my toes, sucking on each one, and curling his tongue around them. He then moved up past my calf, letting his fingers linger as he went. He would make his way to my inner thigh, kissing the flesh closest to my darkness. "Do you like this?" he would ask.

"Yes, yes, don't stop," I'd moan.

"Beg me for what you want," he demanded.

I would be nearly breathless with desperation. "I want you inside of me, please. Please, Stavros, I want you inside of me," I begged as he commanded.

At that point, he would put me in his mouth and lick me with incredible finesse or fill me up with his pulsating hardness. Either way, my climax was always intense, sometimes to the point of almost passing out.

My one-month adventure to find myself turned into a life beyond my wildest dreams—a beautiful, magical fairytale, but one that I had to keep a secret from my parents. Mom would blow the whole thing by trying to weasel herself into what she would think is the opportunity of a lifetime, and Dad, well, I'm not sure if he would be supportive or demand for me to come home since I broke my pledge of sobriety. I decided what they didn't know couldn't hurt them or me.

"Hey, Mom," I tried to sound casual during our bi-weekly check-in while standing outside the villa in my new bikini.

"Hey, sweetie. I miss you. When are you coming home?" The yearning in her voice made me a smidgen homesick. I envisioned her in our kitchen with the peach wallpaper behind her. Undoubtedly, the ashtray would be overflowing with discarded cigarette butts, and sitting next to it was either a cup of coffee or scotch.

"Well, that's why I'm calling. I have some exciting news." I bit my lip and crossed my fingers.

"Here we go," Mom grumbled after letting out a sigh.

"Stop, Mom. I got a job offer to be a hostess in an upscale restaurant. The money they are offering is amazing. They say I look Greek. I guess it's the dark hair and wicked tan, but the fact that I'm American will keep money and customers rolling in. I can totally make bank."

"I was really hoping you were coming home. I miss my partner in crime." She forced a small note of laughter, but I heard something else in her voice that I couldn't pinpoint.

"Can't you be happy for me, for once?"

"I am, but I miss you. Someday, when you have children, you will understand." Her voice was strained.

"I miss you too, Mom, but this is a once-in-a-lifetime opportunity. I hope you'll be okay with it." The guilt that I hadn't felt before was creeping in. Here I was living a secret life of luxury, and she was still singing for her supper.

"Yeah, of course I am, but you'll have to tell your father."

I called Dad next. As soon as he picked up, I heard a baby wailing in the background, and his wife was screaming at him to help her do whatever she was doing. "Yes, sure, honey. That sounds fine," he muttered absent-mindedly before hanging up. I stared at the phone receiver. He didn't even say goodbye.

Many of Stavros' trips lasted for a week or more, leaving me to my own devices. He gave me a credit card linked to his account and full use of the groundskeeper to play chauffeur, as I did not trust myself to go through the mountains.

Many of my afternoons were spent with Cousin Nicholas, who taught me how to free dive properly. I glided through the water like a mermaid. I was becoming one of them. My skin was a deep brown, and streaks of red appeared in my hair. I no longer wore any makeup. It wasn't necessary.

Nick taught me enough phrases of Greek that I could go to the grocery store or pharmacy without having to pantomime. In return, I taught him some English. He was mainly interested in words of the four-letter variety. Sometimes I would catch him staring at me, which had me wondering if he wanted me for himself or was it something else?

Months rolled by with ease. Stavros came and went. Each time returning with an extraordinary gift for me. One month, he brought me a bottle of Caron Poivre. A few months before, a forest green Chanel purse with the signature quilting and interlocking gold C's. I eagerly awaited his return from Russia, excited about what he would bring next. The crunch of the gravel driveway alerted me to his arrival. I ran down the stairs barefoot and threw my arms around his neck. "I'm so happy you're home," I said while smothering his face with kisses.

"What a wonderful greeting." He kissed me on the forehead like my father used to do.

"Oh, come on, you can do better than that." I planted my parted lips on his.

I led him by both hands up the winding staircase to begin my seduction routine. When we arrived at the bedroom, I pulled at his buckle.

"Not yet, my love." He removed my hands from his belt. The gleam in his eye made me suspicious.

"What's going on, Stav?" I patted his pockets.

"None of that, young lady. You will have to wait," he said with a tsk. "We are having a special dinner tonight. Why don't you shower, put on one of the lovely dresses I bought you, and meet me in the dining room at seven o'clock?"

"Okay, but whatever you have up your sleeve, better be good." I turned and went into the bathroom.

Two hours later, I strolled into the dining room to find hundreds of candles flickering in the darkness. The table was covered in rose petals where two champagne flutes stood. Stavros stepped out of the shadows wearing a full black tuxedo, bow tie, and all.

"What is going on here?" I surveyed the room, trying to understand what was happening.

Before I could question him further, he was down on one knee. The enormous stone in the box gleamed, sending flickering colors through the darkened room. It had to be at least two carats and sat on a crown of 18-karat gold.

"Do you remember when you asked me what Eisai o agapinenos mou, meant?"

I shook my head, still dumbfounded.

"It means you are my beloved. I knew it the moment I saw you fall over trying to pick up your ridiculously heavy suitcase. Sarah Caroline, you have stolen my heart. Will you do me the honor of being my wife?"

The fear of living the rest of my life unloved, alone, and broke, was obliterated in that one moment. "Of course, I will."

As Mom always said, 'It's as easy to marry rich as it is to marry poor.'

I was choosing rich.

Chapter 28

OUR WEDDING WAS A small affair. It was only me, Stavros, Nick, and the minister. I wore a white halter sundress that came an inch above the knee. It was a gift from Stavros after his trip to Milan, and he wore a simple blue blazer and ecru trousers.

We stood before the minister and recited our vows where we promised to love one another until death did us part. It was a simple yet beautiful ceremony. We celebrated with sea urchin, lobster, and a salad of peaches, nectarines, and apricots from our orchard.

I did not tell my family for fear that they would ruin it. I imagined Dad standing up and rejecting our union when asked if anyone had any objections because of the age difference and Mom chugging raki until she passed out. No, I wasn't going to let that happen.

Life continued in the pattern we had developed. He traveled, I shopped, and we made passionate love when we were together. It was a simple existence, so simple that after a year, I got bored. When I suggested that I travel with him, he brushed me off with a myriad of excuses.

"I don't want to be alone anymore," I pleaded with him.

"This life isn't enough for you?" His face was taught with anger. "It was welcomed when you were right off the plane. It didn't bore you then," he growled through his clenched jaw.

"That's not fair. You were the one who chased me. I had no intentions of having a relationship with anyone," I lashed back. I reached inside to find the strength I knew I had buried deep down. My body went rigid, and I spoke through pinched lips. "Listen, I'm not sure you understand who you're dealing with. You may have created this fairytale, but I will not be a prisoner like Rapunzel locked up in a tower."

"You are hardly Rapunzel," he sneered. "You are behaving like a child." He flicked his wrist as to dismiss me.

"Fuck you." I stuck up my middle finger and stormed away, leaving him in an echo of footsteps.

Later that evening, Stavros tapped on the door before peeking his head in while waving a white cloth. "I surrender. May I come in?"

I found it exceedingly difficult to deny him. As my defenses softened, our clothes ended up in a pile on the floor.

Our night of passion helped me to win him over. He was finally going to allow me to join him in Athens. We walked off the plane three weeks later into the bustling airport where I had been a lost young American a lifetime ago.

Stavros led me to an idling black Towncar waiting for us when we exited the building. "Eros, I would like to introduce Sarah. This is her first time in Athens." He snickered at our private joke about my awkward arrival.

Eros opened the door, and I slid across the black leather bench. I was giddy as our new adventure unraveled. The city's architecture was much more advanced than I had read at the library. I imagined it would be all ruins. Instead, it was a bustling metropolis with men and women in finery.

"This is incredible," I said in awe as we passed the Acropolis. "Thank you for letting me come." I leaned over to kiss him, but he shook his head.

We pulled up to a high-rise that seemed more suitable for Manhattan, built with shiny steel and tinted windows. As we walked in, heads swiveled in our direction. I held his hand, making sure no one could question whether I belonged.

"Why is everyone staring?" All the eyes cast my way made me feel terribly awkward.

"Because you are so beautiful," he whispered as he ushered me quickly into the elevator.

When the doors parted, we stepped into a massive room decorated in all whites and hues of blue. The floors were shiny marble, with light gray veins throughout. The view in front of us stretched out far above the city.

"Holy shit." My mouth fell open wide enough to catch flies.

"Remember what we said about swearing?" He gave me a sideways glare of disapproval. "You promised to make more of an effort to be more ladylike."

"Sorry, it slipped out. Stav, this place is amazing. I wish I had come sooner." I twirled around in glee.

"Better late than never." He raised an eyebrow. "I need to leave. Make yourself at home."

"I will. After all, this is my home too, right?"

"Yes, of course. The refrigerator should be full. You can always call down to the lobby if you need anything. I will be home very late." He tossed his leather duffle in the bedroom, gave me a quick peck on the cheek, and disappeared.

I sat down on the white couch that didn't have a single stain and took in my surroundings. *Why am I acting so weird? This is your house; go explore.* I did precisely that. I opened the kitchen's walnut cabinets and drawers, wanting to acquaint myself with the apartment. Every single gadget you could need was found inside the drawers. The master bedroom was shocking, with its round bed draped in red velvet under a mirrored ceiling.

I lay on the bed, wondering how many women he'd had in that very spot. Was he watching his performance or that of his companion? The thought of him being voyeuristic was turning me on. I placed my hand in my panties, dabbing at the wetness while plunging the other into my bra. I wriggled and thrust until my body shook in a wave of release.

Stavros came home late, as he said he would, and barely uttered a word. He showered, went to bed, and was gone at the crack of dawn. I was alone again, only in a different location. I decided to spend the day playing tourist. The doorman arranged for a car to take me over to the Parthenon. I walked around, envisioning what life must have been like for Athena, the goddess of war. Men in current times had trouble seeing women as their equals. How did it work all the way back then? I wondered, envying Athena's strength.

The day had gotten away from me, and I was filthy, exhausted, and hungry. I made my way back to our building without incident. As soon as I entered, I was stopped by a stout older gentleman in a uniform. He was not the same man I had seen yesterday or earlier today. "Excuse me, Madam, may I ask who you are visiting?"

"I'm not visiting. I am Stavros Aritis' wife, Sarah." I announced, sounding self-important.

"I'm sorry, you must be mistaken. I have known Mrs. Aritis for years, and you are certainly not her. Perhaps you are confused?" He examined me like I was some crazy person who had wandered off the street.

For a moment, I stopped and questioned myself. Could I be mistaken? Is it possible the last year and a half was a dream? I shook my head to restore my clarity. "Perhaps you are mistaken, old man. I am Sarah Aritis. I have been married to Stavros for over a year, and this is our home. Why don't you go call him to verify? I'm sure he's at his office," I snarled.

With that, the doorman did as I requested. He turned his back to me, not allowing me to read his lips or see his facial expressions.

His eyes were downcast upon his return. "I'm so sorry, Madam. It is my mistake. Of course, you are who you say you are. Forgive me."

I walked away but turned back, recalling his earlier comment. "Who is this other Mrs. Aritis?" I inquired with suspicion. Before he could answer, another resident came in, demanding his assistance with her packages.

Chapter 29

THE PHONE WAS RINGING as I stepped out of the shower. In four giant steps, I closed the distance, hoping it was Stav. "Hello," I answered, still naked and soaking wet.

"Hello, who is this?" questioned the unfamiliar female voice.

"This is Sarah Aritis. How can I help you?" My question was answered with a click.

By the time I had dried my hair and dressed, Stavros had returned home. His hands filled with delicacies. "Dinner, agapi mou," he announced.

"Wow, this smells amazing." I unpacked the bags stuffed with cheeses, fruit, and salads. A scent came from the bottom of the bag that transported me back home to Westfield, as greasy chicken permeated the air. "You remembered." I stuck my head into the bag and took a whiff.

"I thought you might be missing home a little, and this might help. It may not be Kentucky Fried Chicken," he used his best American accent. "But it is Kantuki Fried Chicken." He snorted while making a silly face.

"You are an amazing man, my husband." I leaned into him and placed my hands in his back pocket to squeeze his ass. When I pulled out my hand, a piece of paper dropped to the floor. "What's that?" I bent down to pick it up. Before I read it, he snatched it from my hands and stuffed it back in.

"It's business. Very boring, my dear. Now, where were we?" He took me by the shoulders and began nuzzling the hollow of my clavicle.

"We didn't get a chance to talk about the mirror on the ceiling in the bedroom." I cast him a devilish smile. "Do you like to watch?" I whispered as his five o'clock stubble grazed my cheek.

"Yes, I want to watch as we make love." He slid his hand inside my robe and a finger inside me. "Ah, I see you are ready for me." He moaned.

He picked me up in one swooping motion and stood me by the bed. "Turn around. I want you from behind," he spoke forcefully. Something didn't feel right. Dismissing the nagging pit in my stomach, I leaned over the bed and hiked up my robe, exposing myself to him. I heard his buckle clang as his pants hit the floor. He placed his hands on my hips and glided into me without resistance.

"Oh god, baby. You are amazing." His breath grew quick and his voice intense as he switched from English to Greek. I did not know what he was saying, but he repeated it emphatically until he was spent. Immediately after, he sauntered over to the bathroom and shut the door with a thud.

The unsettling sense that something was off was back again. When he returned, I blurted it before chickening out, "Were you married before me?"

His mouth twitched for a split second before growing into a reassuring smile. "What are you talking about? No, there has only been you, my love." He stretched across the bed and kissed my hand.

I explained my encounter with the old doorman, and he assured me he was mistaken. The Mrs. Aritis he must have been referring to was his mother.

"But you told me your mother died when you were ten." The conflicting stories confused me.

Stavros ranted in a mixture of Greek and English, coming within an inch of my face. "Damn it, Sarah, I have no time for these long explanations of my family history. I have an early flight to Florence to meet with a gold dealer."

I jumped at the rise in his voice. No one had ever yelled at me like that. My dad yelled at Julie, but never me. I followed him into the kitchen. "What's going on, Stav?"

His tone returned to normal, "Agapi mou, you are in a strange country feeling a bit, how do you say, disconnected? Stop creating drama where there is none." He kissed me. "Let's eat some chicken and go to bed."

As my dashing husband slept next to me, his breath was steady, aside from an occasional snore, causing his body to jerk. I wondered how well I knew him. Things had been getting strange since I arrived in Athens. First, there were the stares in the lobby as if I had two heads when we arrived, then being told I'm not who I claim to be by the doorman, the woman who called and hung up, and what about his mother? I remembered the story in detail. He told me she had ovarian cancer and died a slow, agonizing death while he watched helplessly. I distinctly remember him crying as he told me.

In the morning, I waved as my husband left and headed to the phone. One ring, two, three.

"Hey, Squirt." I breathed easier hearing her voice.

"Hey, glamor girl. How is living on a Greek island? Are you making oodles of cash where you work? Meet any hunky guys?"

"Julie, I'm going to tell you a secret, but you have to promise not to tell."

"Sounds juicy. Spill it."

I told her everything about how Stavros and I met, how I came to live with him, and our secret marriage.

"Mom will go bat shit if she hears this," Julie cautioned.

"Listen, I've got more important problems than Mom at the moment." I told her about the strange things that had happened over the last few days. It dawned on me that I had met none of his friends or family other than Nick. He constantly introduced me as Sarah, but not his wife or Mrs. Aritis.

"To quote Hamlet, 'something is rotten in the state of Denmark.' This doesn't sound normal, Sarah."

"I know, right?" I was so relieved to share my suspicions with her.

Julie continued, "If he's gone for the weekend, why don't you snoop around and see what you can find out? He must have a photo album or something. Everyone leaves a trace."

"You're right. I'm going to do that now. Thank you, Sis. You're the best." I hung up with the promise to call her with whatever I found out.

I started in his office. His desk had a glass top supported by short marble pillars mimicking the famous architecture in the area. Behind the desk was a steel three-drawer filing cabinet. I pulled at the handle; it didn't give way. I tried the other two with the same results. "Damn," I muttered. I glanced over at the wall of books on the far side of the room. Brushing my hands over the bindings, I randomly pulled out a few, hoping they might reveal some information.

I was about to give up when I spotted a slight break in the molding surrounding the bookshelf. Upon further inspection, I found a pressure panel, like the ones in the

Colombo detective series. It popped open with minimal force, exposing a keypad.

Significant dates or names that could be swapped for numbers came to mind. Channeling my inner Peter Falk, I tried to break the code. I must have tried twenty different combinations, but nothing worked.

I plonked down on the floor in frustration. While lying on the cold marble, I glimpsed a small piece of yellow paper taped to the underside of his desk. I scooted myself underneath and gingerly peeled it off, hoping not to damage it. It read 7-1-1-6-6. "Bingo!" I shouted, smacking my forehead in excitement.

Exposing the keypad again, I punched in the number, which responded with an audible click. "I'm in." My hands trembled in response to my heart and head's warning.

Inside was a manila envelope with a silver clasp and a brown leather box. I removed them both and placed them on his desk. My throat tightened, making me wonder if I would die right on the spot. I slid the box to sit in front of me. I stared at it for an unknown amount of time, realizing that whatever I found would change everything. If this proved to be a witch hunt, I had wholly undermined our marriage. Any way I looked at it, it was a lose-lose situation. "The truth will set you free," I proclaimed while cracking open the box.

Inside were hundreds of brilliantly cut stones. It appeared to be filled with diamonds, rubies, and sapphires. "Wow," I uttered as the gems dripped through my fingers. Next, I undid the butterfly clasp on the envelope and slipped out the contents.

I found four passports, two with his photo with names I had never heard before, and two with a woman with auburn hair. Her first name was Karen in both passports, and the last names matched Stavros'. *This must be the other Mrs. Aritis*, I thought. I counted thousands of dollars in cash of various currencies, and a black datebook with gold-trimmed pages. Times and dates were written on almost every line.

Adrenaline coursed through my body. I ransacked the apartment, searching for more clues. Who was he, and what the fuck was he doing? Moreover, what part did I play in this secret?

I peered under the bed and stuck my hand between the mattress and box spring, but came out empty-handed. I went through his closet, ripping his shirts from the hangers. I chucked his pants over my shoulder after turning out every single pocket. Inside one of his shoes, I discovered a velvet pouch squished up by the toe. There was a circular object nestled deep inside. I poured its contents into my hand. It was a men's gold wedding band. Inside, the inscription read, 'all my love, forever' in English. *So, he is married or was, to an English-speaking red-headed woman, probably named Karen.* It did not take a rocket scientist to figure out that I was being played.

I may have gotten suckered into a bullshit fantasy, but I sure as hell was going to find my way out. "Know your mark. Get inside their head, and you will always end up on top," my mother's voice reminded me.

My plan required reinforcements. The phone barely rang. "What happened?" Julie asked as soon as our lines connected.

"It is so fucking unbelievable that I'm afraid you may think I'm making it up." I told her about the secret safe and what was inside. When I was finished, there was only silence. "Well, aren't you going to say something?" I screeched as I paced his office like a caged animal.

A deep inhale told me she was still there. "Sorry, I needed a moment to process everything." Julie's voice was replete with sympathy. "Okay, you take one of three approaches. One, you confront him to see if he has some logical, albeit bizarre, explanation for all of this, but I can't imagine he would. Two, you can pack your shit, get out of Greece right now, and come home. Three, you can plot revenge."

"Revenge?" That certainly sounded intriguing.

"Yes, revenge. What if you contacted the local authorities and tipped them off before leaving? Suppose they come and find the forged passports and the jewels? My guess is he would go away for a long time, only this time, it won't be on some cushy Greek island."

"Ooh, who knew you had such an evil streak?"

"No one, and I mean no one, fucks with my family," Julie stated with complete authority.

We planned out every detail. I packed my bags, called the airport, booked a flight home, and pocketed one small diamond for hazard pay. I tucked it inside my bra, under my breast, where it would be safe. After all, I didn't foresee any alimony in my future. It was likely that I wasn't even legally married.

Once I took the last step, there would be no turning back. I called the local police.

"Hello, my name is Sarah, and I believe my husband has committed a series of crimes." I detailed my findings and told them I would leave the door unlocked.

I wheeled my Louis Vuitton suitcase into the elevator; before the doors closed, I took one last look at the life I was leaving. "Mom was right; men suck."

Fifteen hours later, I was back on American soil, where I would have to start all over, yet again.

As I deplaned, my head hung low, and my spirits were even lower until I saw the familiar faces of the people who loved me no matter what.

"Welcome home, Sarah," Julie and Mom screamed as I approached.

I collapsed into their waiting arms. I had never been so happy to be home with The Brennan Girls.

Chapter 30

"You are so tanned, I barely recognized you. And check out that figure. Wow, still a knockout," gushed Mom.

"That's what happens when you live in a tropical climate for a couple of years, Mom."

On the ride home, I let Mom in on the secret Julie and I had been keeping.

"I can't believe you have been gone for so long, and you didn't tell me what was happening. Sarah, you can always trust me."

"Mom, it's only one more fucked up story in a long list of them. Maybe someday I will write a book."

"That, my dear, is a splendid idea."

When we got home, I ran straight to the bathroom to wash away the sheer stupidity and humiliation that was holding my soul in an unforgiving vise.

Stepping into our tiny pink and gray bathroom felt oddly comforting. My muscles loosened a little as I leaned against the door. Relief washed over me that I would be safe. I removed my soiled clothes, throwing them into the white wicker hamper in the corner. As I undid my bra, I heard a ting as something hit the tile.

"Oh shit, I completely forgot." I picked up the sparkling stone. I held it against the light, watching a rainbow of colors bounce around, then hid it in the medicine cabinet behind the vapor rub.

I turned on the water as hot as I could tolerate and scrubbed my skin raw. When done, I tip-toed into my room and climbed into my childhood bed to avoid disturbing Julie.

"Hey, no need to be so quiet. I'm up," Julie said a little above a whisper.

"Jul, can I ask you something?"

"You know you can ask me anything. Remember what Mom always says."

Our voices blended in unison. "We are all we have."

"Seriously, do you ever wonder what you want the rest of your life to look like?"

"Of course. I think about it all the time. All I've ever wanted is to be a mother. Not the kind Mom is, but the kind who bakes cookies and helps with homework. I want to find a man who loves me for me and a little house with a picket fence." Her face was so full of joy as she described her perfect life.

"I have no idea where I'm heading. Whenever I think I'm on the road to somewhere, a major roadblock jumps up and ruins the whole thing. I don't know what I keep doing wrong." My eyes were brimming with tears.

"We Brennan's may not have trouble finding men, but trouble seems to have no problem finding us."

"Isn't that the truth?" I stared at her in the darkness. "You know I love you, right?"

"Yeah, I know. Good night. I'm so glad you are home and away from that criminal."

"Thanks, me too."

Perhaps it was the jet lag, but sleep was not coming. My mind was spinning out of control. I traveled back to simpler times when Dad and I took off and drove together for hours. Then to Jimmy, Stanley, Larry, and

Stavros. The one thing that lifted my spirits was my thoughts of Maggie and her irrepressible laugh.

I pictured her lying next to me in her oversized sweatpants and a ratty old concert T-shirt. The image was so realistic, I could almost feel her head on my shoulder and the weight of her arm laying across my stomach. I missed her down to my very soul.

As quietly as possible, I made my way into the kitchen, took the receiver off the cradle, and crossed my fingers that her mother didn't pick up. "Hello," Maggie's hushed voice answered.

"Hi, I'm sorry to call so late, but I need to talk to you." I slid down the wall onto the cold linoleum floor, curling my knees tightly into my chest, like I used to do when I was a little girl.

We spoke for hours, catching up on the last few years. Maggie's life had not been easy, that's for sure. She still hadn't found a way to escape her psycho, over-bearing mother. After much cajoling, Maggie was allowed out to work, which was her reprieve from the insanity around her. She worked in a small bookstore to lose herself in the lands she dreamed of visiting someday.

"That doesn't sound so bad." I tried to sound supportive. "At least you aren't being held under lock and key anymore." I didn't bother asking if she had anyone special in her life because I knew the answer.

Through the hours, I told her about Stavros, the wedding, the strange incidents that occurred, which led me to be suspicious, and the secret gems and passports.

"Holy shit, that's fucked up." Her voice was a mixture of sadness and anger. "Has there been any news since you left?"

"Yeah, I called the Athens police. I don't want to be peering over my shoulder for the rest of my life."

"And?" She questioned impatiently, waiting for me to continue.

"They arrested him on several counts of fraud and confirmed that we were never legally married."

"Holy shit," Maggie blurted incredulously.

"I am telling you; the truth is stranger than fiction." We laughed a little harder than the moment called for. After a few moments of release, I continued, "Mags, can I tell you a secret?" The question was rhetorical because, of course, I would tell her. I told her everything. I let her in on the diamond I smuggled in my bra. "What should I do with it?"

"Sell it, of course," she blurted without missing a beat.

Chapter 39

THE NEXT DAY, I tucked the diamond back into my bra along with my two-carat engagement ring. I made my way down to the diamond district in New York City, the epicenter of all fine gem trading in the US. Without a clue where to go, I stumbled upon a storefront with a fantastic array of jewelry in the window. Some pieces appeared similar to the items Stavros sold. Wouldn't it be ironic if I sold his diamond to a store that bought his jewelry?

"Hello," an elderly gentleman with ringlets down the sides of his face and a kippah on his head welcomed me.

"Hi," I stammered. "I have a diamond from my engagement ring that I would like to sell and a loose stone that was my grandmother's. Do you buy diamonds?" I had pre-planned what I would say to avoid raising any suspicion.

"Are you joking? They don't call this the diamond district for nothing." His smile was disarming. "Come." He waved at me. "May I see the ring and the diamond?"

I turned my back, reached into my bra to extract the shiny baubles, and handed them over to him.

The gentleman placed each on a scale and then pulled out a loupe to examine the stones. He turned them over while humming and shaking his head. I got excited at the thought of ridding myself of this reminder of Stav. Not to mention getting my hands on some cash to start my life again.

"Did you say these came from two separate places?" His eyebrows drew together, and his forehead puckered.

"Umm..." I was caught off guard. "No, I meant the ring was my mother's engagement ring, and the loose stone was my grandmother's."

"I see. This is strange indeed. I'm sorry to be the bearer of bad tidings, but these are not genuine diamonds. They are synthetic."

"What?" I exclaimed, feeling the blood drain from my face. "What do you mean?"

"Although they are excellent fakes, they are still fake. I'm sorry." He handed them back to me.

I tried to wrap my head around the gem dealer's words. If the diamond or so-called diamonds were fake, what was Stavros doing with a box full of them? Maybe he wasn't a smuggler; perhaps he was a con artist. All at once, everything made sense.

"Oh." I was utterly deflated. "Are they worth anything? What about the gold setting?"

"I can give you one hundred fifty dollars, and that, my dear, is a generous offer."

I took the money he held my way and stuffed it into my pocket.

Shuffling my way back to mid-town, droves of people were moving in herds toward their destinations. Men wore tailored suits with fine leather shoes. The women dressed impeccably in expensive ensembles that looked like they came out of a store window display. Their heels made a quick clicking noise with every step on the concrete. It was as if each molecule of their bodies was supercharged, signaling their success to the world.

Everyone appeared to have somewhere to be except those holding their cardboard signs and a Styrofoam cup, begging for spare change. Dozens of people were sitting in door frames or huddled under blankets on the sidewalk. Contrary to the expensive perfume and cologne drifting about from the beautiful people, the air around them reeked of urine and filth.

I quickly rounded the next corner to escape the overwhelming array of emotions that were tumbling inside of me. In my haste, I stumbled over a lift on the curb, practically face-planting on the ground. From off to the side, I heard a little snicker. I tensed up, ready to give the stranger a piece of my mind, only to find a girl not much older than I, glaring from the alley.

The strange, emaciated waif stepped forward, allowing me to see her yellow smirk and dark, matted hair. The hollows below her dead brown and red glazed eyes were a pale shade of blue. She appeared oblivious to the flies buzzing around the garbage can where she had set up her 'home.'

I stumbled backward, afraid to take my eyes off her. After half a block, I turned and ran the rest of the way back to Penn Station.

Chapter 32

WALKING UP THE LONG flight of concrete stairs to the administration building, young students wearing Seton Hall sweatshirts rushed by with their backpacks heavy with books. All of them acted as if they were late for something or other. I watched them and smiled, wishing I had done this much sooner.

Two hours later, I was formally a matriculating college student. I zeroed in on finance as my major. The stock market was on fire. With President Raegan in office, people working on Wall Street were rolling in money.

'Just say no' was the popular slogan of the times, and that was exactly what I did. I said no to drugs, booze, and men. Instead, I lived at the library for four years, studying everything from English 101 to Global Finance and Investing. I may not have been the brightest, but I had fewer distractions than the keg-swilling undergrads surrounding me, placing me in the top third of my class.

Mom's drinking had gotten a bit out of control, and Julie's love life was erratic, to say the least. She was always in and out of love. Heart full, then heartbroken. My one place of refuge was my phone calls with Maggie. She was the only person who was never disappointed in me. Her faith in my abilities was unwavering.

It was a glorious day in South Orange, New Jersey. The sun shone brightly through scattered paper-thin clouds, keeping the heat down. The stadium was set up for commencement. Rows of chairs lined the field for the graduates, and the bleachers were jammed with family and friends.

Pomp and Circumstance vibrated out of the staticky speakers. I proudly walked with my classmates in our indigo caps and gowns. Who would have ever thought that I, Sarah Brennan, would graduate with honors from college?

Amid the congratulations, I noticed one of my least favorite professors standing next to my father. The nasty curmudgeon of a man made my last semester a living hell. Dad was listening intently while nodding his head. When he saw me, he waved his hand, wanting me to hurry up.

"May I speak with you a moment, Sarah?" My professor's voice crackled with age.

"Of course." I allowed him to lead me to an area with fewer people. *What have I done wrong now?*

"Sarah," he started hesitantly. I braced myself for what was to come. If he followed true to form, he would tell me I had chosen the wrong field. "I have been very impressed with your work this term. You've shown a keen understanding of the material and the maturity to apply it to real-life scenarios." He nodded his head. "If you're interested in a starting position as an assistant to a trader friend, I can arrange an interview."

My jaw went slack. "Are you for real?" I knew he was, but I needed the reassurance.

"Very. At first, this will not be glamourous or high paying, but it will get you in the door."

I thanked him profusely while enthusiastically pumping his hand. "I promise I will not let you down." As we took our leave of one another, he promised to forward my information to his connection, and someone would be in touch.

I walked back to my family and told them the news. We all jumped up and down in celebration.

My graduation was not the only thing we were celebrating. Julie was getting the life she had always dreamed of as a little girl. She had become engaged to Andrew and was to be married in the fall. He appeared to be a decent, hard-working man, but woefully dull. My opinion didn't matter. I only hoped he would give her everything she had always wished for.

I landed a position as an assistant to the head trader. My days were spent fetching coffee, making photocopies, and answering his phone—all tedious activities. But in between, I got to listen to how the business worked. I soaked in any and all information, no matter how trivial.

The trading floor was strewn with little slips of white paper. The traders were frantic as the board changed symbols and numbers. People were sweating and screaming, their arms flailing in the air and their digits flying. It was positively insane seeing grown adults behave in such a frantic manner.

I had been with Gavin, the head trader, for six months before he had an actual conversation with me.

"Sarah, come into my office. We need to talk." He walked into his office without waiting to see if I would follow, which, of course, I did. "Have a seat." He motioned to the only other chair in the office.

I sat down, smoothing my black trousers with my hands, and crossing my legs, intentionally showing my ankles.

"Calm down. You look like you're about to go before a death squad." Gavin took a half seat on his enormous desk.

I took a deep breath to calm down my pounding heart.

"Sarah, you have done an amazing job these last six months. Even when you think no one is watching, I see you absorbing everything around you. You have what it takes to be exceptional at this, kiddo."

I did my best to hide my excitement at hearing his praise. I straightened my posture and let my leg swing a bit, forcing an air of casualness.

"To move to the next level, you must take several tests. Are you familiar with the Series 57, 7, and 63 exams?"

Of course, I knew about the exams, but I never imagined taking them so soon.

"Sarah, I have been in this business a long time and seen people come and go around here. I can recognize raw talent; trust me, you have it in spades."

I studied by night and worked by day. I rarely had enough energy for anything else, but I persevered. I wanted to be one of "them" in the worst way. Within a year, I had completed and passed my exams and officially became a stock trader trainee.

Now, I was not only allowed on the trading floor, but had access to information my previous position denied me. It was no secret that technology was moving at warp speed. Things beyond our wildest dreams were being developed daily. Engineers expected that someday everyone would own a phone that does not connect to a wire, computers would no longer need to dial in for connection, and robots were on the cusp of changing the face of manufacturing. I had no doubt that technology was the wave of the future, and I needed to get in on the ground floor.

Before I approached Gavin or any other traders, I took all the money I had saved and invested in a computer chip company. I tracked the stocks for weeks as they soared. I not only doubled my investment, but tripled it by the end of the quarter. Finally, I would never have to rely on anyone else ever again.

Chapter 33

SUDDENLY, I WAS BOMBARDED with more opportunities than I could ever have imagined. I moved out of our ranch and into my first apartment. It was a small yet charming studio with an exposed brick wall and a view of Columbus Avenue.

After carting all the boxes in, Julie and I sat on the fire escape to smoke a cigarette and sip a couple of cold beers.

"Sarah, this place is amazing. I'm really proud of you." She lifted her bottle in a toast.

"Thanks, Squirt." I rubbed her head in response.

"It's time you stop calling me that." She sounded like she was on edge.

"Hey, what's up with you? Short-tempered much?" I half-joked.

Her carefree attitude turned into one of despair. Her back hunched down, and her eyes glazed over.

"What's going on, Jul? You can tell me."

"It's Andrew. He changed. At first, I thought it was me, but it's not. It's as if he played a game of bait and switch. When I met him, he was perfect. Well, not perfect but perfect for me, but he's become all dark and secretive."

"Could he be a jewel thief or con artist? I only say that because, well, I've been there." I flicked my ashes into the soda can we were using as a makeshift ashtray.

"He's not a con artist." She chuckled. "But something is going on, and I will get to the bottom of it."

"If you need any help, say the word, and I'll come kick his ass." I wrapped my arm around her shoulder in sisterly solidarity. Julie spent the first night with me, but after that, it was all mine.

I continued to bust my ass at work, knowing I still had so much to prove. My stocks were soaring, but I wasn't ready to cash out yet. Once I shared my investment strategies with Gavin, they promoted me. I no longer actively worked at the trading desk. Instead, I oversaw the brokers of my company, giving them insight into the patterns I had been monitoring in the ever-changing world. My new office was on the seventh floor of one-forty Broadway. One of the finest financial addresses in New York. I celebrated by tossing out the Louis Vuitton suitcase Stavros had given me and bought an even bigger one with my very own money.

Next, I purchased a beautiful co-op on the Upper East Side. My new one-bedroom home was on the thirty-seventh floor of a doorman building with views of the East River. It was spacious by New York standards. I kept the decorating minimal: white walls and black furniture accented with chrome tables and lamps. It was a far cry from the brick ranch overflowing with tattered furniture where I grew up.

My job kept me busy and out of trouble. Any financial insecurity I had as a child evaporated as my bank account grew. Dad had moved south, but we spoke daily on my walk home. I spent the time regaling him with stories of my latest victories, hoping I was making him proud.

Mom and I spoke on Sunday mornings before she started drinking. Anything later than that was a gamble, and anything after seven was useless.

One rainy Thursday, my umbrella flipped inside out on the way home, leaving me exposed to the elements. Once on the other side of the door, I tossed out the broken umbrella and dropped the drenched briefcase in the sink. As I padded into the other room, the phone chimed.

"Hello," my voice sounded as annoyed as I felt.

"Oh, I hope I didn't interrupt something fun," my best friend had a devilish tone in her voice.

"No such luck. I literally walked in the door right this second, and I am soaked to the skin. Can you hold on while I strip and grab a towel? It's freezing."

"Of course. I'll enjoy the visualization," Maggie said in her throaty voice.

I stripped naked, wrapped a large towel around me, and put the kettle onto boil. "I'm back. Sorry about that."

With a warm cup of tea, I curled up on the couch to continue our conversation. She told me about the latest New York Times bestsellers her store was stocking. Which books were worth reading, and those that were not. I kept my report basic to not rub in the fact that my life was continuing as hers was stagnant.

I knew it was a longshot, but I invited her to New York City to visit. Secretly, I hoped she would say yes, and I would be able to convince her to stay. She shot down the idea straightaway. There was no way to escape her mother's talons.

"Can you come here?" she suggested. "You could visit the store, and we can spend a little face-to-face time. And boy, do I miss your face."

"I would love to, but I recently got promoted, and Julie is pregnant. I need to be here for her. Her husband is turning out to be a huge asshole. I can't leave. As soon as I'm settled in and I know Julie is okay, I'll come visit. I promise."

Chapter 34

THE FOURTH ROUND OF shot glasses was lined up across the bar, filled with tequila. "Hey everyone, raise your glasses," Gavin yelled over the crowd. "Here's to Sarah." He raised his hand. "Her killer instincts and drive to succeed are unprecedented. Happy birthday, Killer; I can't wait to see where this year takes you. This bitch might end up ruling the world." Everyone raised their glass, threw back the shot, and howled Happy Birthday.

The tangy lime still tingled my lips when I sensed someone standing behind me. I turned around quickly to chastise the person intruding on my personal space. I raised my hands to begin my tirade, but I recognized his eyes before the first word came out.

"Funny running into you here,." He extended his arms to receive a hug. His ebony hair was cut short, showing off his stellar cheekbones, and his dark, brooding eyes swam under the neon lights.

"Oh my god," I screamed, entering his embrace. "What are you doing here?"

"This is my haunt. I live right around the corner." Robbie shook his head in disbelief that we were face to face.

"Geez." He moved me away so he could give me the once over. "Seems you've done very well for yourself."

I spun around, wobbling a little in my high heels. He steadied me with his hands.

"I guess Nurse Ratchet and the rest of the motherfuckers in Rochester let you out," I said, louder than intended.

"Shh." He put his finger to my mouth, trying to quiet me.

I responded by taking his finger into my mouth and sucking on it.

He pulled it out, wiping the wetness on his shirt. "Sarah, how about I take you home, and you can fill me in," he whispered so close to my ear that his warm breath danced on my skin.

My body spontaneously reacted to his offer by setting the tiny hairs on the back of my neck on end.

"Sure, let's have one more drink." Turning back to the bartender, "Hey Scotty, line them up and an extra one for my dear friend Robbie." Grabbing him by the face, I planted a wet kiss on his mouth with a lip-smacking, "Muah."

In the morning, my stomach rebelled against the remnants of the alcohol in my system. I sipped at the glass of water beside the bed tentatively. The clock read 10:45 am.

"Here, these might help," said the voice coming out of the shadow, offering two white chalky pills. I looked at him quizzically. "Don't worry, it's only Tylenol," he assured me.

I swallowed them down and collapsed on the pillow with a groan.

"Looks like you're hurting today," Robbie offered sympathetically.

It wasn't a dream, I thought, cracking open my eyes. I tried to sit up but failed. "Robbie, how did I get here?"

"I brought you home. I was afraid to leave you in that condition. A girl like you could get into a lot of trouble in a state like that." He raised his eyebrow in disapproval. "I hope you don't mind, but I helped you out of your clothes. They didn't seem very comfortable." He turned slightly pink with embarrassment.

"No, not at all, thanks." I cupped my eyes, trying to see, but the sun was blinding. "I can't get up yet. Why don't you lie down next to me and tell me what you've been up to for the last however many years?" I patted the empty space on the mattress.

He complied with my request.

"So, tell me everything," I demanded. "I have all day."

"Well, after you left rehab, I went really dark, like bottomless pit of hell dark. I was alone, again." The sadness I had become so acquainted with in rehab was back and had taken over his face.

"I'm sorry," I said, holding his hand.

"About a month after you left, I was sitting on that old rickety bench you and I hung out on, replaying all our conversations. I finally realized you and the therapist were right all along. I was being pig-headed. It would be impossible for me to have a life if I didn't work through my grief, anger, and guilt. It wasn't only that my mom and dad were killed in the fire. It was that I wasn't home to save them. If I hadn't been at that stupid party, my parents might still be alive." He shook his head, reliving the horrible memories. "I was carrying a lot of guilt. Sarah, I was a fucking mess. I'm glad they didn't let me go any sooner. I probably would have gone back to using."

"Are you clean now?"

"Mostly. I still drink, but I keep it in check. How about you?"

"Same here. I keep myself in line because now I have so much more to lose."

"You can say that again." He glanced around in awe. "It sure beats my dump, but I have one thing that you don't."

"Oh, really?"

He piqued my curiosity. He flipped through the notepad beside my bed and scribbled an address on an empty sheet. "Meet me here at nine tonight." With a kiss on the forehead, he was gone.

All the ingredients for my hangover concoction were in the fridge. The ginger, cucumber, and apple went into the blender, and then I fried up an egg sandwich with sausage and cheese. Within the hour, the headache and nausea subsided. Next, I rolled out my yoga mat and pushed through a few vinyasa flows to start my sluggish blood moving.

I arrived at the address promptly at nine o'clock to find Robbie sitting on the steps of an old brownstone amid a littered street. He was very handsome in his cargo pants and collared shirt.

He jumped up as I approached. "Hey, so glad you made it. I thought you might stand me up."

"Nah, that's not my style," I assured him with a peck on the cheek.

Taking me by the hand, we began an ascent up six flights of stairs. I stopped on the fourth floor, gasping for breath, holding up my hand, indicating I needed a minute.

"Don't quit on me now. We're almost there."

Finally, we reached the top. I leaned against the wall as he opened the door, revealing a scene straight out of a romantic movie.

White lights lined the perimeter, giving the roof a moonlit glow. A small garden table with a white tablecloth and two chairs sat in the corner. "Welcome to my favorite spot in Manhattan," he burst with delight. It was apparent he put a tremendous amount of effort into the evening. A deliciously rich scent wafted through the air as he lifted the silver lid from the serving tray, uncovering the coq au vin.

"Wow, this is wild. I've been to many fancy places, but this, by far, is the best." My hand was covering my mouth as I was taking it all in.

"Why, thank you, Madam. May I pour you a glass of champagne?" He tipped his head and gave the smallest of bows.

After a couple of glasses of champagne, Robbie was struggling with his thoughts. "Sarah, there is something I think you ought to know." His eyes were downcast, and his voice trembled.

"What is it?" I asked cautiously. The air was heavy as I awaited his revelation.

"After I got out of rehab," his voice drifted off, and his leg began to shake the way it had done years before, "I spent some time in jail."

My eyes grew wide. "For what?" The Robbie I knew wouldn't hurt a fly.

"It's not as bad as it sounds. I didn't hurt anyone or anything like that. It's just that I didn't have any money, and an old high school buddy told me of a way to make some easy cash. It was dumb." He shook his head. "There is no such thing as easy cash." He chuckled at his gullibility. "Anyway, this guy told me all I had to do was walk into a bank, tell them I wanted a mortgage, and show them some fake ID he supplied for me. He said it would be easy, and no one would ask questions because all my paperwork was 'as legit as you could get.' The next thing I knew, there was a crazy banging on my door. Sarah, I was terrified. The cops threatened to kick down the door if I didn't open up." His leg was shaking like a jackhammer instead of an appendage.

"Oh my god. What happened next?" I was breathless with anticipation.

"Well, I thought about climbing out the window, but I've watched enough cop shows to know that it wouldn't end well, so what else could I do?" He shrugged. "I opened the door. They threw me on the ground, kneeled on my back, put me in handcuffs, read me my rights, and tossed me in the back of a cop car. I have never been so scared in my life." A trace of panic changed his features as he relived the past.

I shifted my butt to the edge of my seat to listen even closer as the story unfolded. My hands braced my chin as I leaned in.

"As it turned out, the whole thing was a setup, and they made me the patsy to take the fall. They gave me two years in a white-collar prison since I had no priors, and it was a non-violent crime."

"Holy shit, Robbie, this is crazy. Are you making it up to get sympathy points?"

"Hand to God, Sarah. I shit you not. The upside is that's where I learned to cook. When I was little, I loved helping my mom in the kitchen. We made chocolate chip pancakes every Sunday morning." I watched as he had drifted off to another time. "Mom would make the batter, and when we were done, she would ask, 'Chips in the hand?' and pour me a handful. God, I loved her. Anyway, when I got to the prison, they asked what skills I had, so I told them, 'I can make a great chocolate chip pancake,' and that was it. They assigned me to KP duty. It was not too bad. I learned to make kick-ass beef stroganoff and a cheesecake that would knock your socks off."

He regaled me the rest of the evening with stories of celebrities who taught jailhouse yoga and children of stars with whom he played basketball in the courtyard. He made me crack up so hard that I had to cross my legs to not pee myself.

Once Robbie was released, he went to live with his aunt and uncle in Brooklyn and got a job as a sous chef in lower Manhattan. After a few years, he was able to afford his own place. It wasn't fancy, but it was his.

Somehow, our chance encounter in a bar blossomed into a loving and easy relationship. The kind he had hoped for so many years before.

Most nights, when his shift was over, he would knock on my door and climb into bed. Our lovemaking was comfortable and safe.

Until our pillow talk changed one winter night. "Sarah, we would have the most gorgeous babies," he cooed, pushing the hair away from my eyes. "They would be smart too, like you," and he kissed me on my nose before heading off to the shower.

The thought of being a mother had never occurred to me. I had my sights set on conquering the world the last few years, and the idea of a baby made me feel... well... normal.

The next step in our relationship occurred so gradually that he was living with me before we made a conscious decision to do so. It was merely a formality when he brought the rest of his possessions and slipped his clothes into the drawers I had emptied for him. As he unpacked, I wondered if he was finally 'the one.' Once the last of his belongings were unpacked, he turned around with a small velvet box in his hand and dropped to one knee.

"I know it's not much and not what you deserve, but would you do me the honor of marrying this poor hack from the wrong side of the tracks?" He grinned while opening the box.

Inside sat a sweet gold band embedded with three petite emeralds.

Looking at the ring and back at him, I found myself mute.

"I hope you don't hate it." His eyes begged for affirmation. "I bought it at an antique shop. It reminds me of one my mother wore."

"Oh no, I don't hate it at all. It is lovely." As he slipped the ring on my finger, a dozen questions and doubts ran through my head. Without giving him an official answer, Robbie picked me up, laid me on the bed, and made love to me while I wondered why I didn't say no.

I lay awake, staring at the ceiling, my thoughts darted in all directions. The illuminated numbers on my nightstand read eleven o'clock. I left Robbie sleeping peacefully to sit in the living room. I stared at the phone, wondering if it was too late to make a call.

The phone rang only once before an irritated voice answered. "Hello," she barked. "This had better be an emergency to call someone's house at this hour."

"Hi," my voice sounded so small. "I'm really sorry to call so late. This is Sarah. I'm a friend of Maggie's."

"Any friend of that Jezebel is a heathen. Don't let me catch you calling here again." The phone slammed down.

Our wedding was a small ceremony held at the New York City courthouse. It was the two of us, Julie, Andrew, Mom, and Dad. I wore a crème-colored satin dress with a plunging neckline that perfectly framed the petite diamond necklace I had purchased at Tiffany's. The three-inch Christian Louboutin stilettos were the pièce de résistance. Robbie was very handsome in the black Armani suit with the matching cream-colored tie and pocket square I bought for him.

As we waited for our turn, Robbie's leg did the jig that gave away his state of mind. Slow meant he was calm, but eager. If it quickened, that usually meant his anxiety was ramping up. I caught Julie's sneer of disdain she was casting our way.

"Sarah, can you come to the bathroom with me?" she said, meeting my glare with equal emotion.

"I'll be right back," I shouted over my shoulder. "Don't go anywhere." I gave Robbie a wink and one of my award-winning smiles.

"I'll be right here waiting for you," Robbie stated dutifully.

Once the door shut, Julie leaned against it to ensure no one else could enter unannounced. "Are you sure about this, Sarah?" she pleaded.

"What? What are you talking about? Is this retribution for me not liking Andrew when you married him?"

"Of course not. I would never be that petty," Julie barked. "I'm your sister and have had a front row to your life. I've seen you in love, like real, I'm going to love you forever love, and I have seen you in a dog in heat kind of lust, but I don't see either of those things when you look at Robbie. Whatever it is you feel, I don't think it's marriage love."

My temper began boiling up like a teakettle about to whistle. "Little sister, listen to me." I grasped her wrists. "I had my one shot at love with Jimmy, and that will never happen again. I've come to accept it. Sometimes you have to adjust your expectations," I preached. "Robbie loves me. He needs me, and that puts me in a position of power. You and I both know that's what it's all about." I turned away to check my makeup one more time. In the reflection, I read the sadness in my sister's eyes. She had always been a dreamer, but dreaming is for suckers. "Now, please, shut your trap and be my matron of honor." I slid my arm through hers, guiding us through the door.

We walked out as our names were called by a stout woman wearing reading glasses held on by a long, beaded string.

"Ready troops?" I corralled my merry band of family, leading the charge into the Justice's chambers.

We gathered in a semi-circle. Robbie and I held hands as we exchanged promises of love and devotion in sickness and health.

"Should anyone present know of any reason that this couple should not be joined in matrimony, speak now or forever hold your peace."

"If I may interject," said my mother.

"For fuck's sake, Mom."

She always had to ruin everything.

"I know I should have said this before, but I need to say it now. Robbie, my baby, has been through enough. I hope you're aware of how special she is."

Robbie nodded in agreement.

"You are not to hurt her. Do you understand?" Mom warned him.

"Yes, Ma'am," he stammered.

"And don't call me Ma'am. You can call me Jackie or Mom, but not Ma'am," she scolded.

We made it to, "You may kiss the bride," and with a wave of relief, I was married... again.

Chapter 35

I WAS SURE THAT this time my marriage would stick. After all, Robbie was an honest human being with a sweet disposition. He loved me before I made my money, and even if I didn't feel exactly the same way, I took comfort in having his warm body in my bed at night.

The first year of marriage glided by without a single argument. When time allowed, we did all the things young married couples do. We sat on the couch eating pizza and watching old movies. The kind Mom and I used to watch. We hung out on the fire escape, smoking cigarettes until the sun came up, lost in easy conversation. Most Sundays, we explored the city, holding hands while strolling through Central Park.

I spent over sixty hours a week trying to make my department the most profitable and well-run in the company. Robbie and I moved into a more spacious apartment on the Upper East Side, befitting our upwardly mobile lifestyle. I loved not having to ask anyone for anything. The sense of independence was liberating. I called the shots in my life and most everyone else's.

Several months after the move, it was a sunshiny New York City Sunday. The streets were teeming with people leaving church. The sidewalks were littered with tables and chairs set out for brunch. It was our second anniversary, and all was right in my world. As we were making our way down Fifth Avenue, a beautiful smokey gray flannel suit in the window of Brooks Brothers caught my attention. "Oh, Robbie, you would look dashing in that." I pulled him lightly by the arm. "Come on, let's go in."

"Sarah, I don't want to do this. You know stores like that make me uncomfortable." He broke free of my grasp.

"Don't be such a killjoy. Please, let me spoil you a little. Consider it an anniversary gift." I begged. Head tilt, hair strand, crooked smile.

"Sarah, please listen to me. I don't have the money for this place, and I don't like you flaunting yours. It makes feel like a loser." Even though he was standing still, his leg bounced.

"You, my dear, are not a loser. I only want to show you how much I appreciate you." I nibbled at his earlobe.

"Stop that. What the fuck are you doing?" He barked and stormed off.

Running after him, I grabbed his arm, spinning him around. "What's wrong with you?"

"Me? What's wrong with me? You've got to be kidding me." He was exasperated. "You walk around all high and mighty because you have some fancy job that pays you tons of money, and you entirely disregard my feelings. I'm the man in this relationship." He pounded on his chest like Tarzan. "How the fuck do you think it makes me feel that you pay for everything? It is downright degrading," he snarled.

"Hold on." I held up my hand to stop him. "I'm lost. When did all this happen?" I was blindsided by his tirade.

"Of course, you never noticed because you're never home. When you're not at the office, you're on the phone with work, talking about work, or doing work. I'm your houseboy and sex slave, nothing more."

"This is all so fucked up. Thanks for a shitty anniversary. Don't wait up." It was my turn to storm away, leaving him on the street with his ridiculous leg shaking.

I found myself standing in front of my office building. Passing through security, I flashed my credentials and got into the first elevator that arrived. As soon as the steel doors shut, the first tear fell. "Stop it, Sarah," I reprimanded. "Pull it together." Before the doors reopened, I composed myself and strolled down the hallway.

My corner office had a wall of glass overlooking the street. I stood with my arms wrapped around myself, attempting to make sense of what happened. At a loss, I picked up the phone.

"Hey, Squirt, how's it going?" I was trying to sound nonchalant.

"What's wrong?" She noticed everything.

"When you were having those problems with Andrew, did you ever figure out what it was?"

"Not really. I'm still getting the run-around. Things are still pretty bad. Why?"

"Because something bizarre just happened with Robbie." I described our fight in detail. "So, what do you think?"

"It sounds to me like he's a tad bit insecure. You guys didn't talk about money before you got married?" She sounded surprised.

"No, it never occurred to me. I mean, Dad told me to have a prenup signed, which I did, but other than that, I didn't think my money would be a problem. He certainly didn't mind living the high life when it suited him." The irony of this statement was not wholly lost on me.

"Sarah, I think you should hang up the phone and go home. He's the one you need to be speaking to." I could hear in her voice she was holding something back.

"Go on. What else were you going to say? I can hear it in your silence."

"Please don't take this the wrong way, but try not to throw the money thing around. I hate saying this, but you have gotten a bit full of yourself."

"Whose side are you on?"

"Always yours. If your sister can't be honest with you, who can?"

It took a few beats for me to answer. "I don't like what you said, but there may be some validity to it. I'll think about it. Thanks, Squirt." We were about to hang up when I remembered, "Hey, sorry, I'm all twisted up. How is that deliciously delectable nephew of mine?"

"He's my saving grace." Her love seeped into the words. "He is my favorite human in the world."

"How's Andrew?"

"A douchebag."

"Well, then I am doubly glad you have Baby Jack. Give him a kiss and a squeeze from his Auntie Sarah. If he were any sweeter, he would give me a cavity. Have to run. Love you, sis, and thanks."

As usual, she was right. I hung up and worked my way back uptown, trying to unscramble my thoughts and figure out what to say when I arrived. I found it inconceivable that he would resent me for making more money than him. When we met, I was making six figures. Did he think that was going to change magically?

I ran all the different scenarios in my head. I needed to be prepared for whatever was going to come my way.

"Good evening." Max, the doorman, touched the brim of his black cap as I entered.

"Hi, Max. Did you see Robbie come in?"

Max swiveled his head back and forth to the elevator, his forehead furrowed in concern. "Yes, ma'am. He came in about an hour ago."

My hand trembled as I put the key in the lock. I steadied myself. "Robbie?" I called out, not seeing him in the living room. "Honey, we need to talk." Making my way to the bedroom, I had to step over piles of clothes scattered across the floor. "Robbie?" I called, picking up his underwear.

"Oh my god! Are you fucking kidding me? In my house? My fucking bed?"

Neither of them moved. On my mahogany bedside table was a small bag, a lighter, and a piece of aluminum foil. She still had the tourniquet tied around her arm.

"Get the fuck out of my house." I went full crazy on her, grabbing her long blonde hair and pulling her naked body out of my bed. She moaned as she hit the floor. "Get the fuck out of my house, you fucking junkie," I demanded, giving her forceful nudges with my foot.

Realizing it was useless, I sat in the living room to wait them out. The two of them were so high that the building could be burning, and they wouldn't move.

My real marriage turned out to be no more successful than my fake one.

Chapter 36

I MUST HAVE DOZED off because the bleach blonde bitch was sneaking out the door when I woke up. A minute later, the sliding door of the shower rattled open. My next step would have to be very calculated. Entering the bathroom with the stealth of a cheetah, I leaned against the double sink, staring at his silhouette as the shower stall fog thickened, obscuring me from sight.

His voice echoed in the oversized bathroom as he sang the most recent Sinead O'Conner hit. The door opened once he sang the last verse, releasing all the pent-up steam. He flinched at the sight of me. "Holy shit, you scared the crap out of me." His voice was a higher pitch than usual. "When did you get home?" He tried his best to sound nonchalant, but the quiver in his voice couldn't be hidden.

"Last night." I kept my tone even and unemotional.

"I can explain," he babbled.

"This should be interesting."

He stepped out of the shower and wrapped a towel around his waist.

"Oh, don't cover up for me. I've seen it all before and got an eyeful yet again last night when you were laying spread eagle on my bed, stoned out of your fucking gourd with that bitch."

"Can we not do this here?" He pleaded while making his way back into the bedroom. He sat on the edge of the bed, and his leg began dancing.

"How long? How long have you been using?"

He didn't answer. He repeatedly dragged his hands through his hair, and his leg was going full jackhammer.

"How long," I insisted.

"What the fuck do you care?" His pupils were like pin dots. "You're always at work, and when you're here, you treat me like I'm your pet instead of your husband," he fired back. "You don't even see me. Don't you get it? You fucking bitch. This is all your fault." He shook a cigarette out of the pack on the dresser and lit it to buy time. "Sarah, you were the one person in my life who understood me, but you've changed. You got all this money and prestige, and there's no room for me."

"You are a weak, pathetic little man. Grow some fucking balls and talk to me. What, do you think I'm a mind reader? So, instead of acting like a grownup, you start screwing other women and doing drugs?"

"Fuck you, Sarah," Robbie hollered, his eyes glossy with tears.

"I will not feel guilty for being successful. I hit rock bottom too many times to go back now," I screamed in indignation. "Yeah, I have money and success, but I have earned each and every penny with my blood, sweat, and tears."

"Yeah, I'm sure you fucked your way up the corporate ladder."

The sting of his skin against my hand sent a shock wave through my system.

"What the fuck, Sarah?" He held his hand on top of where I had hit him.

"Leave my house now and don't ever show your face around here again. We are done."

He snatched his underwear and jeans from the floor and headed out the door. "By the way, I understand why your father bailed. All of you are bat shit crazy. You, your mom, and your bastard twisted sister. You're all fucked up."

I threw a glass at him as he left, but unfortunately missed. "Don't let the door hit you on the ass on the way out," I bellowed as the door slammed shut. "And don't come back."

When I was sure he was gone, I dead bolted the door. Next, I used the intercom.

"Hi Max, this is Sarah in 3712; please be aware that Mr. Sutton is no longer welcome in my home or this building. If he shows up, you are to call the police. Do you understand?"

"Yes, Ma'am," came the crackly reply.

Frantically, I ran around my apartment, throwing out everything that had to do with him. The drugs went directly into the plastic sack, as did his cologne and all his clothes. By the end of the day, I didn't want a single trace of him left behind. It would be as if he had never existed.

Once I was done, I collapsed on a chair. "I will not cry," I told myself repeatedly as I poured another glass of scotch. "I will not cry."

The phone rang. As soon as I heard, "How's my girl?" I fell apart.

Sobbing uncontrollably, I uttered the words, "I need you, Daddy," through gasps.

"Sweetie, calm down. I would be there if I could. Tell me what's going on." The concern in his voice made my heart calm down a bit. I wiped the snot dripping from my nose on my sleeve and dried my tears with the bottom of my white silk shirt.

I told him the entire sordid story, heroin, and all.

"You did the right thing, baby. He's not worthy of you. I didn't like him from day one, but you would have been furious with me if I said anything."

"Of course, I would be angry; I'm a grown woman. I am successful and liked, and... and..." The waterworks began again. "Dad, I don't understand what I keep doing wrong. How do I always end up alone? The whole time growing up, Mom said men were assholes, and she was right."

"Stop right there. Your mom is not right. She has a very skewed view of relationships. Listen, sweetheart; there's a lot about your mom that you don't know. She didn't have an easy childhood."

"Since when did you start defending her?" I scoffed.

"Sarah, your mom and I have an extremely complicated relationship, but trust me when I say we have never stopped loving each other. Once upon a time, we created a family, which will keep us bound forever."

"Wow, this is the first time I'm hearing you speak about Mom that way."

"Maybe if I had been more present and more verbal, you would have had a better role model." His voice dripped with regret. "Princess, I wish I had the answers, but I don't. I think it's time for you to talk to a professional."

"A shrink? Dad, I've already done that. I talked to Elaina at rehab day in and day out. There is nothing left to discuss."

"But you were still a kid then. You're an adult now with adult problems. You need someone to walk you through this. I don't want you to end up on drugs again, which can easily go that way. Your mother should be your cautionary tale. I don't want that for you. Do you?"

"Thanks for the vote of confidence." The smell of the scotch in my hand caught my attention. I walked over to the kitchen sink and poured it down the drain.

Cradling the phone receiver between my head and shoulder, I opened my desk drawer, rifling around for the little white business card I had stowed away years before. I found it dog-eared and creased.

"Thank you, Dad, for talking me off the proverbial ledge."

"I'm always here for you, darling. You are my sunshine."

Chapter 37

I PACED AROUND THE apartment, canvassing each room, seeing ghosts of the past everywhere. I envisioned him making love to me in the bedroom. It was as if I was watching it on television—his body braced over me, regaling me with his visions of our future.

"Baby, with your brains and my street-savvy, we will take on the world." He raised his brows and squinted his eyes in a mockingly sinister way. "Donald Trump better look out because I am making love to the next multi-millionaire." Then he kissed my neck and clutched my breasts. Closing my eyes, I could almost relive the sensation of my body coming alive with his touch.

Memories lingered in every room. In the kitchen, nude except for the strings of an apron tied around his neck and back. His high, tight baseball player's butt was perfection. In fact, his entire body was damn near flawless.

I sidled up behind him and wrapped my arms around his waist, dipping my hand down further. "Stop that, or breakfast is going to burn."

"Let it burn, baby. I know exactly what I want to eat." I dropped down to my knees.

I was caught in a cycle of memories. I sat down on the floor and smashed the back of my head against the white lacquer cabinets until I was dizzy. When I stopped, I glanced at the wedding photo hanging directly in front of me. "No fucking way, buddy." I pulled the silver frame off the wall and dropped it into the garbage.

I scrubbed every inch of my place. Every floor, counter, and chachka, determined to clean even the tiniest trace of his existence out of my life. My hands were raw and stunk of bleach by the time I was finished. "Fucking great! Now my manicure is ruined," I screeched, kicking the empty bucket. I was covered in sweat and filth. No matter how clean my apartment was, it would always be tainted by the memory of Robbie.

"Jesus Christ, I can't take this anymore," I hollered, throwing the sponge against the white wall. The time had come to pull up my big girl pants and call her.

"Hello," said the familiar voice with a British accent.

"Hi Elaina. It's Sarah Brennan."

I could envision her grandmotherly eyes lighting up. "Oh, my dear Sarah. 'Tis so wonderful to hear your voice."

"I'm sorry it's been so long."

"I figured everything was going swimmingly when I didn't hear from you."

"It was. At least for a while. Elaina, I need some help. Do you have time to talk?"

"Of course, that's why I gave you my home number."

With each tale of woe came the familiar, "Please continue" or "Uh-huh." Elaina never interrupted when her patients were on a roll.

When I finished, she asked the question I had been waiting for, "Are you using any drugs as a coping mechanism?"

"No, I'm not," I swore emphatically. "I am drinking, but not as a painkiller, I swear. I have it under control. I'm sure I wouldn't be calling you if I didn't." The thought of my past drunken behavior with men made me cringe. "Elaina, I finally have something to be proud of. No one would have ever believed that I could have done this." I scanned my apartment with a sense of awe and pride. Everything was mine. "But I have this overwhelming foreboding that my life is a house of cards that is about to come crashing down. Oh god, Elaina, I'm at a loss. Please, help me."

Elaina asked me to return to Rochester, but not to the center this time. She invited me to her home for private sessions. Besides my and Robbie's brief honeymoon, I hadn't taken a single day of vacation. A few weeks' respite was long overdue.

Before we hung up, I asked Elaina why she had given me her home number.

"I had a niece once. She was beautiful and intelligent, with all the potential in the world. Still, like you, she came from a less than traditional family. Her self-destructive behavior ended up killing her. When I see the despair in your eyes and hear the heartache in your voice, I am reminded of her. Perhaps if merely one person showed her kindness or glimpsed past her rough exterior, she might still be alive. My heart breaks that I was not in England to assist with alleviating her pain, but I am here for you."

I curled up on the sofa like I used to in Elaina's office and pulled the throw blanket over me. "I'll call you tomorrow to update you on my arrival. Thank you, Elaina. You are my savior."

"Oh no, Sarah, you're saving yourself."

Chapter 38

THE DRIVE NORTH BROUGHT back the memories of my darker days. The ones I thought I had outgrown. Once I passed the "Welcome to Rochester" sign, the pit in my stomach became almost untenable. My hands were shaking so hard that I found it difficult to control the steering wheel. *Deep breaths in, deep breaths out*, I reminded myself for the rest of the drive.

I reserved a room in a bed-and-breakfast on the outskirts of town. A half-dozen pigmy goats were grazing on the deep green grass in front. They were no bigger than the average size dog. I carefully parked my car to ensure not to injure the lovely creatures.

"Well, hello, cutie pie," I addressed the goat closest to me and received an adorable bleat in response. I scratched my new friend behind the ear.

"Hello," came a voice in the distance. The older couple hurried toward me. "Welcome to Strawberry Fields."

"Thank you. I'm so happy to be here."

"You must be exhausted from your trip. Let me show you to your room. Honey, can you take her suitcase?" Mrs. Rigby called over her shoulder to her husband.

"Right-o," he saluted without missing a beat.

I wondered if they represent what it was to be happily married. Could that kind of relationship be a real thing?

We walked into the white two-story clapboard farmhouse, which was as neat as a pin, so the saying goes. On our way to my room, she stopped at the slate mantel with a dozen photos perched upon it. She beamed with pride as she told me who everyone was. Mr. and Mrs. Rigby had four children and twelve grandchildren. Each image displayed people of various ages smiling and holding each other.

"What a beautiful family you have." I absentmindedly caressed the picture frame.

"Thank you. They are my pride and joy," she cooed. "Thank goodness they all stayed in the area. My babies and grandbabies are my everything." She held an adjacent photo as if love itself was wrapped around it.

We walked toward the back of the house, passing through the kitchen; I noticed a glass-enclosed porch that showcased their expansive property. The lush green trailed off into the horizon.

"It is so beautiful here," I spoke without intending to.

"I must say, I agree. This is my slice of heaven, and the goats are my friends. If you'd like to come out to feed them with me in the morning, you are welcome. You would be hard-pressed to find anything cuter than a pigmy goat in the morning."

"That sounds amazing." I smiled at the memories of my time with Star.

"Let me show you to your room. Right this way." She held her hand out to allow me to pass. The evening light filtered through a sheer gauzy curtain. I was surrounded by antiques that had to be a hundred years old. An enormous sleigh bed covered in pillows of assorted sizes and colors was in the middle.

"I think you should find everything you need right here. The desk has paper and pens in a drawer, the switch for the fan is next to the bed, and fresh towels are in the bathroom. We serve breakfast from seven to nine. Please help yourself to anything in the fridge. Our house is your house." She grinned, exposing her slightly crooked teeth.

I gushed on and on in appreciation of the last-minute accommodations.

"Our pleasure. Any friend of Elaina's is a friend of ours."

I unpacked all my belongings and laid down, sinking into perhaps the most comfortable mattress I had ever been on. I pulled out my newly acquired cell phone to call my sister. Who would have ever thought we would be able to walk around with a phone in our purses? I did, that's who. I held out the small device that made me a fortune. Before I dialed a single number, I drifted off with my clothes on and the phone open in my hand.

In the morning, the sun awoke me like a gentle kiss. I stretched and glanced at the clock; it was seven-thirty. Being out of Manhattan and away from all the stress gave me an organic high. I showered and threw on my most comfortable jeans and my old red checked flannel shirt to go out to visit the goats.

The air was crisp for a September morning, and the scent of the leaves changing mingled with the breeze. As I stood observing the goats, Mrs. Rigby appeared next to me with steam rising out of a hot coffee mug featuring Ringo Starr.

"For me?" I sighed.

"Milk and two sugars. I hope that's okay."

"Perfecto. Did I miss the goat feeding?"

"Yes, dear. We feed them at six. They'll still be here tomorrow." Her voice was cheery and light. "Now, how about some breakfast? I can make you an omelet, or how about some cinnamon French toast? It is my specialty."

"That sounds heavenly."

"Give me a half-hour, and breakfast will be served." With a pat on my shoulder, she was gone.

I strolled around the pen, watching my little friends jostle each other around, imagining how easy it would be to live somewhere like this. I took a deep inhale of the country air and closed my eyes to let the sun dance upon my upturned face.

A terrible cry came from the house, causing me to spill my coffee. I ran inside to investigate, praying no one was hurt. When I entered, both Mr. and Mrs. Rigby were staring at the television with their mouths agape in horror. On the screen was the image of one of the World Trade Centers, with smoke billowing out of it.

"What in God's name is going on?" I shouted. "This can't be. It isn't possible." I shook my head, unwilling to believe the videos running on a loop. I darted out of the room, picked up the phone. My hands were trembling to badly that it took three times to punch in Julie's phone number. She picked up on the fourth ring.

"Hello," her voice showed no sign of strain or fear. She didn't know.

"Jul, where's Andrew?" My voice quaked.

"He's at work. Where are you? What's wrong?"

"I'm in Rochester. Turn on the news."

"Listen, I'm feeding Jack. Can this wait?"

"No, turn on the news right now," I demanded.

The next several hours were torture. I waited for word from my brother-in-law and my colleagues. Almost everyone I knew was in lower Manhattan. I lay on my bed, glued to the news reels until I dozed off. The vibrating of the phone woke me up some time later.

"Hey, Sarah. It's Gavin." At the sound of his weary voice, I sobbed.

"It's okay. We're okay."

"How can you say that? Nothing is okay. What the fuck is happening in the world?" I continued to sob.

Gavin recounted what had happened a few hours prior. All the staff were accounted for. Everyone was covered in soot, but made it out alive. Many were struggling to find ways home, but those who lived in the city took them in. The world was in chaos.

"This is America. These things don't happen here." I was still shaking my head in horror.

"That was before. Everything has changed. This is a pivotal moment in history. Everyone will ask, where were you when the Trade Centers fell? Sarah, this changes everything."

"Gavin, you sound strange. Are you okay?"

"No, not really. I'm glad you aren't here, and there's no need to rush back. It will take some time to figure out what will happen next or when we'll be able to occupy the office again. Lower Manhattan looks like a war zone." The tone of his voice terrified me.

The aftermath was splattered all over the television. It was impossible to comprehend how something like this happened.

"Sarah, I've got to go. Stay where you are until you hear from me. Okay?"

"Yeah, okay. Thanks for filling me in."

By the end of the day, I found out all my nearest and dearest were safe, but thousands of lives were lost. I'm sure I partied with many of them or sat next to them at conferences. My heart crumbled as I recalled a private party I had attended at The Metropolitan Museum of Art thrown by Cantor Fitzgerald. It was a spectacular evening celebrating the Rodin sculptures donated to the museum. The tuxedo-wearing staff passed Champagne and hors d'oeuvres as we strolled from room to room, viewing the art. I stood mere inches from some of Monet's most famous masterpieces. At the time, I wished Julie could have experienced it with me.

As that evening progressed, I wound up at the Temple of Dendur, where a live band played rock hits from the previous decades. Everyone who was anyone attended, and so did I. That was the night I knew I had made it.

I wept for all the souls that perished and the families in mourning.

Chapter 39

IN THE MORNING, I drove into a quiet suburban neighborhood. The lots of land were small, manicured squares of perfection. Beautiful elm trees lined the road, giving the perfect amount of shade.

Before getting out, I double-checked the folded piece of paper I held in my hand. Twenty-six Stafford Drive, the note read. Upon the fence post was the house number scrolled out in fancy calligraphy. *Ready or not, here I come.* A lovely brick herringbone walkway led up the porch of a charming pale-yellow colonial. On the steps sat pots of burnt umber chrysanthemums. I took a lap around the block to clear my thoughts before climbing the stairway. There was no doorbell, only a brass knocker in the shape of a sun. It emitted a dull "clack, clack, clack," when the hammer hit the strike plate.

The door opened within moments. Elaina stood in the morning sunlight wearing a light pink knit cardigan and thick cream corduroys. Over the last decade and a half, her once blonde hair turned gray, and she appeared to have shrunk an inch or two.

"You are a sight for sore eyes," she said, taking me into her arms.

I hugged her back and didn't want to let go.

"Come on into the study. I have some tea and a cozy fire waiting for us," she said as we detached. The rooms we passed through appeared how one might imagine an English cottage to be decorated. The last door in the hall led to a small wood-paneled den with a stone fireplace. She decorated in much the same manner as her office had been some years ago. The navy blanket I often crawled under in her office was draped along the back of the sofa. "Go ahead; I brought it here for you."

I sat down and wrapped the softness around me.

"Yesterday must have been horrible for you," Elaina started.

"I can't even begin to process everything yet, but my family and colleagues are safe."

"Thank goodness. It will take time to come to terms with what has happened. Do you want to discuss it?"

The unfathomable that occurred would have to wait for another day. "I don't think I'm ready for that yet."

"I understand." She poured us tea and handed me the lovely porcelain cup with a pale purple forget-me-not pattern.

"My grandmother had this same pattern."

"Did you like being with your grandmother?"

"Not particularly. She was extraordinarily critical, sometimes downright mean. I was always reprimanded for having my elbows on the table or using the wrong fork. Nothing I did was ever right. Whenever I went to their house, all I wanted to do was go home. I understand why my mom hates her." Glancing around the room, a warmth radiated within me. "How is it that being with you makes me feel at ease?" I questioned.

"You are asking a very important question." Her accent was still thick. "Let's start with that."

"So much for the catching up before heading straight in."

"We have plenty of time for that later, but let's start here; explain to me what you are feeling physically, right at this very moment."

I took a minute to mentally survey my body. "My muscles are relaxed. I feel like I could curl up and go to sleep in front of the fire like a cat."

"Why do you think you have this sense of calm?"

"Hmm." I mulled it. "Being with you makes me feel like I can completely be myself. You don't want anything from me, so I'm free to drop my guard."

Elaina nodded, indicating I was on the right track. "Very interesting. Can you recall feeling like this at other times in your life?"

"How do you do that? I haven't even been here a half-hour, and you already have me peeking into my dark and twisted places."

"I'm not asking you to go anywhere you haven't been before. I am only asking you to talk about it out loud," she elucidated. "It's like when you walked up to my house. What did you see?"

"I saw a house with a red brick walkway and flowers on the step. I saw a front porch with white wicker furniture."

"What emotions were evoked when you saw these things?"

"Anxiousness. Fear."

"When you came inside, how did you feel?"

"Relieved."

"Sarah, that's what we're doing. We are going inside your house. From the outside, we have so many questions. Why? How? When? What if? But when we are inside, everything becomes clear. It is not so much why something happened; it's more accurate to ask how we move forward from here?"

I returned to Elaina's every evening for two weeks. We spent hours by the fire, sipping tea like old friends and shining a light into my soul to put the past to rest. By week three, the pieces were fitting together.

"Sarah, let's talk about the relationships you've had over the past ten-plus years. What commonalities do you see when peering from outside your house?" Elaina continued, using the metaphor we had been working with.

"They are all very handsome with forceful personalities. They were all very sexy in their own way." I bit my bottom lip, thinking about their physical characteristics.

"How did each of these relationships end?" Elaina inquired, even though we had previously discussed the details ad nauseam.

"Relationship-wise, Larry was a fling. He really wasn't any different from the guys I had been with before. That being said, I was outright devastated when he told me he couldn't keep me on at the ranch. I loved living in Sedona. Stavros was a criminal. I was so blinded by his charm, dashing good looks, and the fantasy of it all that I ignored the obvious. I have no doubt he was setting me up to take the fall for something. As for Robbie, I recognized something wasn't right, but I desperately wanted to love him and make our relationship work. He seemed like the easy answer."

"Does that ring any bells with you?" She raised an eyebrow.

"No. Should it?" I shrugged my shoulder in confusion.

"Let's peer inside your house, shall we? Who is the one constant male figure in your life?"

"My father."

"Tell me about your relationship with him?"

"It's good. My father and I are super close. He always gave me money, took me to rehab, and bought me a car."

"Sarah, I am sure your father is a decent guy in your eyes, but let's peel back the surface and discuss what's beneath. Your parents divorced when you were a young child. From the stories you have told me, he has left you repeatedly throughout the years."

I took a moment to go through my mental Rolodex of life events to see if I could find any substance to what she was saying.

She spoke softly, "Sometimes people will gravitate toward the type of relationships they've had in the past, even if they were not the healthiest. Suppose your relationship with your father was traumatic or, in your case, perpetually disappointing, you may be more likely to choose a partner who will disappoint you in much the same way. For some, it's because that was what they experienced growing up, so this is the type of relationship they seek out. For others, having a partner similar to the parent is an unconscious, desperate hope of gaining that parent's love. Does any of this hold any truth for you?"

I sat stunned at the words that rolled off her tongue. How did I not see it? "This is all about him, isn't it?"

"Yes, and no. He is the key to opening the door. You are now free to roam the rooms of your house. Sarah, in identifying the patterns with the men you've chosen, you'll be able to free yourself from the past. It's time to stop fighting upstream and claim what is rightfully yours.

"You are not your mother, nor are you daddy's little girl anymore. You do not need your father or any man to define you or give you validation. The decisions you make now are for Sarah, the adult. The intelligent and generous person you have become. You do not owe anyone anything."

Chapter 40

I LAY IN MY countryside room ruminating about the past, watching the fan continue its rounds. The blades never stopped spinning. They simply did their job, going around and around, making no forward progress. I, too, was caught in a perpetual cycle of men that leave me emptier than when they found me.

I walked over to the oak desk and examined the homework Elaina had assigned. It had three columns with headings: healthy, unhealthy, and abusive. I slid open the drawer, removed the pen with the Strawberry Fields logo, and circled the most applicable ones for each man.

When I was done, I stared at the completed chart. I hadn't put a single check in the healthy column, not even for my father. As an afterthought, I added one more name.

The following day, Elaina opened the door with a welcoming smile. "Good morning, Sarah. Please come in. It's getting chilly." She tightened her beige cardigan snuggly around her.

We settled into our usual spots with our tea set out on a tray. I was the one to open our morning conversation.

"I worked on the chart you gave me last night. At first, the results startled me. I never thought of myself being in unhealthy or abusive relationships. I certainly didn't view my relationship with my father that way. The more I thought about it, the more I comprehended he was physically absent most of the time. Sure, he showed up for the more significant events, but always left quickly. He threw money at me to relieve himself of his feeling of guilt." Like in the Sunday comics, I felt like a lightbulb popped over my head. "He always left. He left me behind. On the day he moved out, I begged him not to go. I promised to behave, but he left anyway." I was fighting back the tears. "Elaina, I wasn't enough. I'm never enough." My tears would no longer be denied.

"It's okay, Sarah, let it all out. This is one of the scars you have been carrying around for decades. One of the most profound feelings of sadness is being abandoned by those you love, and you have had more than your fair share of loss. I am going to go make us some more tea."

When Elaina returned, much of the fog had cleared. I raised my floral cup, took a sip of the aromatic peppermint tea, and closed my eyes. "I'm okay now," I assured Elaina.

"Are you ready to continue?"

"Yes. Some things are coming together."

Elaina used her hands to motion for me to continue.

"Last night, I added one more name to the list."

Elaina's eyebrows raised inquisitively.

"What if the only time I was in a healthy and loving relationship was with a woman?"

"Go on," she prompted.

"We checked all the 'good' boxes. She was my friend but became so much more. I can't believe how blind I've been. Boy, talk about looking for love in all the wrong places."

We both laughed.

"Every day, we can write a new chapter to our story. We have a choice. The question is, are you ready to choose to put yourself in the driver's seat of your life, or will you allow the past to navigate?" Elaina challenged.

Chapter 49

I PACKED UP MY car and hugged Mr. and Mrs. Rigby goodbye. Before pulling away, I rolled down my window. "You say goodbye, I say hello."

She put one finger on her nose, pointed the other at me, and blew me a kiss. "We'll miss you. All of us, the goats too."

With one final wave, I was gone, traveling back down the well-worn dirt road toward the highway.

The closer I got to the city, the more on edge I became. My breath became shallow, and my thoughts were everywhere all at once. It became increasingly clear that my arrival back in New York would not be light and breezy.

After parking in the garage, I walked in to find Max still standing guard by the front door. "Hello, Ms. Brennan. Welcome home."

I wrapped him in my arms—something I had never done before. Standing back, I studied him. He had changed. The city had changed.

"Are you okay, Ms. Brennan?"

"Yeah, I suppose I am. How's your family?"

"Fine, thank you. We are all doing okay, but you should know that your neighbor, Mr. Burns, was lost."

My jaw went slack at the news.

"He was on the path train heading to New Jersey to visit his mother. The train didn't make it out of the station."

A single tear escaped. I closed my eyes to regain my composure so I could continue without falling apart. "Thank you for telling me. When you have the chance, please find out where I can send flowers?"

"Of course. I will have the information to you by tomorrow."

"Thank you, Max, and if I haven't said it, you do a remarkable job." I slipped him a one-hundred-dollar bill before heading upstairs.

Returning to my apartment was like walking into a carnival fun house, where things are not always what they seem. All the ghosts of the past still lingered in the air, distorting my reality. "I am not home," my words echoed in the apartment.

I ran a hot bath, letting the lavender salts melt, and added a teaspoon of bubble bath. While waiting for the water to fill, I went to the kitchen and brought out one of my Waterford wine glasses. Opening the refrigerator, I reached past the chilling bottle of wine, took a seltzer out, and poured that into the glass.

I climbed into the bath, letting the warm water help release the tension in my muscles, and I closed my eyes. Over the next hour, I figured out what I needed to do.

In the morning, I began sorting and sifting through everything. I would only take my most personal possessions, and the rest would be disposed of or given to charity; I didn't care. Everything spoke to the person I never wanted to be but still became.

The dull ring of my doorbell alerted me to a visitor, which was strange since I lived in a secured building. Julie stood on the other side of the peephole with Baby Jack in her arms.

"Oh my god, how did you get up here?" I cried out as I flung open the door.

"Max let us up. I told him I wanted to surprise you." She glanced around at the assorted piles. "What's going on?"

"Come, sit down and I will tell you everything, but first, give me that boy." I cradled Jack in my arms and smothered him with kisses, to which he responded with squeals of joy. "I missed you, Squirt, and you too, handsome little man."

"Are you always going to call me that?"

"Yup," I jabbed while giving Jack belly kisses.

"What's going on here? Are you going somewhere? Again?"

I ignored the sardonic tone in her voice. "Jules, I'm leaving. I'm going to move upstate. I can't do this anymore. For years, I've been miserable. My therapist and I agree it is time for me to make a change. I am choosing me."

"Yeah, okay," Julie scoffed in a snotty tone, taking Jack back as if being with me would somehow contaminate him.

"What?" I was flummoxed by her response.

"You've always chosen you. Dad has always chosen you. Mom has always chosen you. How the hell is this different? It has always been about you. I am so sick and tired of it."

"What the fu—" I stopped because I noticed Jack was taking in every word. "What's your deal? I thought you would be happy for me."

"Oh yeah. You take off, Dad takes off, Grandma and Grandpa leave, Mom is so fucking drunk she's barely aware of what day it is, and my marriage is in shambles. Please, go find yourself." She stood up, tucking Jack on her hip. "Safe travels," she shouted as she walked toward the door.

"Julie, please don't leave like this. I am not deserting you. I can't breathe here. This is not the life I want, and if you don't want your life, do something about it. Leave Andrew. He's an asshole, no different from the rest of them, but don't blame me for his shortcomings."

"I can't leave. I have no one and no money of my own."

"That's not true. You have me, and I will give you any money you need," I insisted.

"Thanks, but I'll be alright. I always am. Not everyone needs to run away from their problems. Some of us face them dead on, but thanks for the offer."

We hugged at the door, silently comforting each other. Without saying a word, we both understood that neither of us was living a happily ever after. I had to save myself, and she would have to as well.

My first call was to my attorney to get the ball rolling on the divorce. With the prenup in place, and our marriage being as short as it was, Robbie didn't have a leg to stand on to ask for alimony, or anything else for that matter. All assets were in my name.

The next call was to the realtor, who helped me purchase my apartment. She was at my door with the listing papers in hand within an hour. Once fully signed, I packed up my car, turned the engine, and headed out of the city. I did not look back. Not so much as a glance.

Chapter 42

THE WIND WHIPPED MY hair as I drove north on I-87. I cranked up the music to the point the steering wheel vibrated in time with the bass and sang along with Melissa Etheridge at the top of my lungs. My body relaxed into a posture of ease. The last time I had that sensation was when I was riding Star. The further north I got, some of the trees started to change color.

I stopped twice during my almost six-hour drive. The first was for a value-sized cup of coffee to keep me going to my destination. The second was to relieve me of said coffee. Once I crossed the town line, I pulled out the slip of paper tucked into the outside pocket of my purse. Two-forty-seven Maple Street was scrolled on a small piece of paper I had ripped from the pad near my desk. On the back were directions on how to get there.

I zigzagged my way through the streets while taking in the majestic mountains that were everywhere. Circling the lake, I made my way into the quaint downtown. The streets were lined with sweet mom and pop shops selling everything from knitting supplies to organic pet food. I was surprised places like that existed outside of postcards and movie sets.

To the left was the outstretched red awning with the store's name and logo in white print. Pulling down the vanity mirror attached to the visor, I refreshed my lipstick and ran my fingers through my hair. "This is as good as it's going to get." I snapped the mirror closed and stepped onto the street. With no cars coming, I crossed and peered into the window. I counted to ten and opened the door. The little bell attached to the handle announced my arrival.

"I'll be right with you," called out a voice.

"Take your time." My heart was beating so quickly that I could hear it pulsating in my ears.

She stopped what she was doing and turned around. Her eyes grew to a size that I would not have thought was humanly possible. "Oh my god! Am I hallucinating?" Maggie squealed.

"No, you're not. Sorry, I'm so late. I got sidetracked for a few years. Forgive me?"

In two strides, she stood in front of me. Her chestnut hair was in a French braid, and she wore little to no makeup. The sight of her took my breath away. Impulsively, we leaned in to embrace, but she froze and backed up. Maggie's change in demeanor spoke to her fears.

Once her shift at the bookstore ended, we met up at an adjacent coffee shop, where we tucked ourselves into a private corner, away from prying eyes.

"What are you doing here?" she probed, still in disbelief.

"I came here for you. I didn't realize it, but it has always been you. I am so sorry it's taken me so long. Maggie, you are my very reason for breathing. How fucked up is it that our time in rehab truly was the happiest I had ever been in my life? No man or amount of money has ever fulfilled me the way my time with you did. I was in denial." I reached out my hand and took hers.

"Stop. You can't do that here. If my mother finds out, I am out on my ear. No questions asked. I may be an adult, but make no mistake, I am a prisoner." Her face was etched with terror.

"Maggie, listen to me. I'm here now. You can be free. That is, if you still want me." When she didn't respond, my face fell, recognizing that I may have read the situation wrong. "I am so sorry, Mags. It didn't even dawn on me that you wouldn't want me. It was arrogant and downright rude of me to show up the way I did." I took my hand back and cradled my teacup.

"I do want you with me, but my life is not my own. While you were out in the world figuring everything out, I was stuck here. My world is ridiculously small. It is me, my books, dinner with mom, and off to bed. I'm afraid you'll be disappointed. I'm not the same girl you once knew."

When I gazed into her eyes, it was clear as day. She had been broken.

"How about you let me decide?" I asserted. "I understand this seems very sudden, and I don't want to spring everything on you at once, but I am ready. I'm ready for you. Ready for us. If you'll have me."

Breathing the same air as Maggie and having her within inches was more intoxicating than any drug. After two hours, we laid out a basic plan to implement. First, she had to go home and pack. I offered to go with her but was refused, claiming it would only add fuel to the fire. We would meet at my hotel when she was done.

I paced the hotel room for hours, then tossed and turned in bed. My imagination was going wild. The stories she told me sent shivers up my spine. She certainly would have been in protective services if she had been a minor.

Time passed incredibly slowly, and all I could do was wait and pray. Each minute that passed had my imagination going wild with worst-case scenarios. When the last one included Maggie's mother killing her, I decided to go to her house. I couldn't wait anymore.

As I was about to open the hotel room door, there was a quick succession of raps. From the peephole, I saw it was Maggie standing with her back to me. I opened the door and led her inside, grabbing her suitcase before closing us off from the outside world. When she turned around, an imprint of a hand against her cheek leaped off her tearful face, and her left eye was quickly turning purple.

"Oh my god. I knew I should have gone with you. Maggie, are you okay?"

"I will be." Her sobs began to subside once in the safety of our room.

"I'll be right back." I snatched the ice bucket and the key to the room, hoping I would be quick enough to keep the swelling at bay.

When I returned, I found her staring out the window with her back to the door. "I have lived here all my life and never saw the town from this angle. It's kind of beautiful." Before I had a chance to speak, she continued, "I've spent my entire life searching for ways to escape. Drugs, running away, even attempting suicide. When none of that worked, I gave up on any thoughts of happiness. You coming here for me is beyond surreal. I am so afraid that I will wake up, and this will all have been a dream."

I came up behind her and took her hands in mine. "It's not a dream." I kissed her behind her ear. She let out a small gasp, which I took as a sign to continue. I kissed the nape of her neck, working my way down. Once her shoulder was free, I kissed her there too. I advanced slowly, wanting to savor the moment. Her back arched as she leaned into me. I turned her around, tenderly kissed her, and then continued to rediscover the woman I had become familiar with many years before.

It took us hours to explore each other's bodies. Every nook and cranny was touched, kissed, or stroked. When we were done, we lay in bed, gazing into each other's eyes.

"You have no idea how many times I've fantasized about this, Sarah. I spent so many nights wondering where you were and hoping you were thinking of me, too. I have to confess, I thought you considered us just friends."

I draped my arm around her naked waist. "Honestly, I did think of you as a friend, my best friend. I supposed I didn't want to admit that the one night with you opened me up in a way I hadn't experienced before. Once you left, I shut that door and locked it. I didn't know what it meant. After working with Elaina for a few weeks, some unresolved feelings resurfaced. Once they did, I couldn't and didn't want to deny them anymore. After all, men weren't working out for me." I winked.

"Yeah, I guess I ruined you for everyone else." She batted her eyelashes at me.

"Yes, you certainly did." I kissed her on the nose, a feeling of contentment washing over me.

Chapter 43

WE WORKED OUR WAY out of bed, showered, and went out for dinner. Before we walked into the restaurant, Maggie took me aside. "Sarah, I need you to act like we are friends. No touching. Not until we're out of town. No one can know about us." The ease of the previous few hours had disappeared, and her anxiety had crept back in and taken hold.

"Good evening, ladies. May I offer you the wine list?" the waiter proffered a small leather-bound book with a smile. His eyes grew large, and his lips turned down when he saw Maggie's swollen face and black eye. She quickly turned away from the candlelight, blocking his line of sight.

"No, thank you. Sparkling water will be fine," I answered for both of us. When the server walked away, I said, "I hope that's okay with you. I'm not drinking anymore."

"Yes, totally fine. I have no reason to escape reality because this is a dream come true. I don't want to ruin it. So, what do we do now?" Her lips were slightly parted in a delicate upturned arc, and her eyes sparkled in the candlelight.

Without thinking, I stretched my arm across the table, taking her hand and interlacing our fingers. Maggie abruptly pulled it away, placing it under the table. "I'm sorry," panic rose in her voice. "I can't. Not until we're out of here." Fear was always her companion.

"In that case, we'll leave first thing in the morning." I smiled. "Leave everything to me."

The world was still dark when I woke up. I was too excited about what was to come next to sleep. I propped myself up on my elbow and studied her face. She now had a few small creases next to the corners of her eyes and a few gray hairs near her temple. Nothing anyone else would notice, but I knew they were there. I wanted an intimate knowledge of each crease, hair, and freckle. The sun crept in as it rose, shining its light across her face, accentuating her beauty.

"Good morning, sleepyhead," I whispered with a kiss. "Time for us to hit the road."

"Where are we going?" insisted a slightly grumpy Maggie.

"First, we're getting you coffee, so you become human, and then we'll have three hours to discuss."

After grabbing a couple of cups of our magic elixir, we hit the road.

"So, are you going to tell me where we're going?" Maggie gave me the side-eye.

I only hoped she was as excited about what I had put into motion as I was. "I can tell how much you loved the bookstore where you worked, and I love you and books," I spoke while waving one hand around in the air and steering with the other. "Since you basically ran the place, I thought we might open our own bookstore and coffee shop in Great Barrington, Massachusetts. Have you ever been there?"

She chuckled with a crooked smile. "The only places I've been are rehab in Rochester and home. Do not pass go, do not collect two hundred dollars." I loved her little Maggie-isms. "And no, I do not know where Great Barrington is. Not to mention, how are we going to fund this little dream of yours?"

I gave her a sly glance out of the corner of my eye. "Didn't I tell you I was loaded?"

"What? Like *loaded* loaded, or we'll scrape by and pray the store takes off kind of loaded?"

"*Loaded* loaded. You know I've been managing a trading floor, right?"

"Yeah, sure, but I don't know all that much about finance or business." She shrugged her shoulders.

"Well, it seems I have an innate instinct for tech stocks. I invested in a couple of chip companies. The kind that go into computers, phones, and stuff, not the potato variety."

We both giggled at my silliness.

"I was making a sizable salary, so I took most of it and invested, and well, it paid off, big. In fact, you could say huge."

"Shit, Sarah, are you serious?"

"Dead serious. We have seed money for the shop and enough for a little house if you want."

As I drove seventy miles an hour, she kissed my cheek. "Count me in."

For the rest of the ride, we verbally sketched out how we would like the store layout, what kind of coffee and pastries to serve, and, most importantly, what we would name it. All that was left was finding the correct location.

Three and a half hours later, we were rolling down Main Street. "This looks oddly familiar." Maggie surveyed the area with a crinkled nose, which I found very endearing.

"That's why I picked it. You will find a similar architectural and historical vibe to Lake Placid, but this place is way cooler. We'll be accepted here. It's hippy central. Peace, love, and all that jazz."

"I never thought of myself as a hippy, but I like it." She gave my hand a tight squeeze.

Once we checked into the small inn on the far side of town, we strolled down the street and into the first real estate office we came upon. An older woman with long white hair and a smocked pink shirt was sitting behind the desk. Our initial consultation was quick, and she didn't bat an eye when Maggie and I held hands. My lungs felt as if they were expanding for the first time.

Our new real estate agent, Peggy, informed us that an old house had been converted into a store on the corner of Main and Church Street in the heart of town. She took a key off the hook and led us to the property. We stood on the sidewalk examining the cedar-shingled two-story house with a front porch. There were two bay windows, making it easy to imagine the book displays that would entice those walking by to stop in.

Everything about it spoke to my soul from the first step through the door. An elegant antique bronze chandelier was hanging from the ceiling with incredible stained-glass shades. Two-inch wide oak molding ran through the perimeter, and beautiful red oak floorboards were below our feet.

I could almost smell the pages of the books dangling in the air and the murmur of our future patrons. Maggie was biting the inside of her cheek, trying not to give away her excitement, but we both sensed what the other was thinking.

"It's perfect," I called over to Peggy. "Let's draw up the lease."

Maggie and I embraced, freely and without judgment, for the first time in public.

Peggy smiled warmly. "Why don't you stay a few more minutes and meet me in the office when you're done? I will start the paperwork." She called over her shoulder as she left, "Don't forget to lock up. Welcome to Great Barrington."

"Thank you!" we squealed in unison.

Chapter 44

THE FIRST TWO MONTHS were frenetic. The floors needed to be sanded and refinished, the walls painted, bookshelves and displays built. Not to mention the café portion, which would require electricity, running water, tables, and chairs.

"Sarah, what would you think of having a small area in the corner with a couple of couches? We could ask local writers and poets to come and speak. Or," she rattled off ideas so quickly, I thought she would burst, "what about musicians? We can have an open-mic night. Also... how about a children's hour? We can have story and craft time." Her brain was working on overdrive. Everything about her was alive and filled with hope. She was back.

Four months later, the red ribbon draped across our door was cut by Mayor Allen. At that moment, Sage's Pages and Cafe was officially open to the public. The townspeople streamed in to explore the latest addition to the village. People milled through the displays, picking up books with jackets that called to them with their vibrant colors. The fresh-brewed coffee wafted out from the café on the notes that Herman strummed. His song selection struck a sentimental chord, as they were the same songs my mother sang when I was a kid.

Our store was a warm and nurturing place where everyone could be at ease. It was a judgment-free zone. *I made this*, I thought with overwhelming pride. I caught a glimpse of Maggie speaking with Peggy. *Correction,* we *made this*.

As I chatted with customers, I sensed someone watching me. When I turned around, it was none other than Elaina. I squealed as if a little kid was given a pony. "Oh my god," I shouted. "I can't believe you're here. Oh gosh, I think I might cry." My eyes welled up with tears.

"I hope those are tears of happiness," said Elaina.

"Oh yes, absolutely. I'd like you to meet Maggie." I waved my arm, beckoning her to my side.

Maggie glided effortlessly through the crowd, charming everyone as she passed.

"Honey, I'd like to you meet someone very important to me. Maggie, this is Elaina. Elaina, meet Maggie."

"Hello Maggie. Sarah has told me so much about you. Would you mind if I gave you a hug? I consider us practically family."

"Of course. You are responsible for bringing Sarah back to me. How can I thank you?"

"No, thanks required. Love one another. Take care of each other. You have built something exceptional. I am so happy for you both."

An impish face poked out behind Elaina. "All You Need Is Love," interjected Mrs. Rigby.

We all burst into a fit of laughter.

The opening day was coming to a close, but I had one more thing to do before our guests left. I stood in the front of the store and rang a silver bell to grab everyone's attention. Maggie peered on from the café.

"Hello, everyone. On behalf of Maggie and myself, I would like to thank you all for coming. Since our arrival, the welcome we have received has been nothing short of incredible. We could not have picked a lovelier place to call home. Which, by the way, if anyone is selling, we are in the market to buy," I mentioned with a chortle. A few people raised their hands. "Okay, let's talk afterward," I responded. "Opening Sages Pages has been an amazing experience. I would like to make today even more special. If you will, please indulge me for a moment."

Everyone was perplexed, including Maggie.

I stepped behind the counter that held the cash register and opened it. I took out what I was searching for and hid it behind my back. "Maggie, please come up here."

Maggie checked around to see if anyone would clue her into what was happening, but everyone appeared as baffled as she did. She put down the espresso she was in the middle of brewing and made her way to me.

"The woman standing beside me has a heart of gold. She has been my rock through some of my darkest times. She has been my friend, my confidant, and my lover. She is all the things I have been searching for all these years. I don't know why it took me so long to see it." I turned to Maggie, whose face was shining like the sun. "Maggie, my love, would you do me the honor of marrying me?"

Everyone in the store erupted in cheers and applause.

Above the din, she screamed a resounding, "Yes."

I slipped on the one-carat brilliant-cut diamond I had specially made at the same store I had visited years before. Though a fake diamond represented my fake marriage, this one was very much real.

That night, as we lay in bed, Maggie fingered her ring, spinning the glittery circle repeatedly. She had a sparkle in her eyes as she played with it. "Sarah, I would give anything to marry you, but the law does not recognize same-sex marriages, as you are well aware."

"I understand, but I won't let the government tell me who I can marry. I have been married to men, theoretically legal, and they didn't work. We will be married in the eyes of God, and that's all we need. Eventually, the government will catch up, and when that happens, I would be thrilled to marry you again." I stroked her milky white arm dangling from her oversized Harley Davidson T-shirt.

A few months later, we purchased the sweetest cape cod with white clapboard siding, black shutters, and a front porch where a swing rocked in the breeze. The living room had a massive stone fireplace with an oversized wooden mantel that commanded the attention in the room. I loved it because it made me think of Elaina. The views of the valley were a prism of greens and amber, and the fragrance of grass perfumed the air.

We cultivated a small garden where we grew our own wildflowers and vegetables. Neither of us knew anything about gardening, but thankfully we owned a bookstore where we could find all the answers.

Chapter 45

I NEEDED TO CALL Julie, but the thought of how it might play out was terrifying. I desperately wanted her to be happy for me, but I also knew she would be pissed. I could only hope she had come to understand and had forgiven me. As the phone rang, I paced the living room, while intermittently holding my breath. I froze as soon as the ringing ceased.

"Hey, Squirt," my greeting was slightly above a whisper.

"Look who it is," she quipped sarcastically. "I wasn't sure I would ever hear from you again."

"I'm so sorry. There is no other way to say this, but I had to save myself, and the only way was to cut all the ties. I didn't cut ties only with you. I haven't spoken to Mom or Dad either."

"Yes, I am well aware, since they ask me daily where you are and if you're okay. As if I would have a clue."

"I really am sorry that it played out this way. I'm calling with happy news and an invitation." I tried not to sound angry, but was gnashing on my lower lip.

"That's awesome, Sarah. You keep taking off and then reach out when things don't work out or when you fall in love." She sniggered. "What? Did you get married again?"

"Funny you should say that." I went on to tell her about my history with Maggie and how we found each other again. I told her about Sage's Pages and the wonderful friends we had accrued during the last two years.

"Once again, my congratulations Sarah. You really aren't very good at being alone, are you?"

"Lose the tone, Julie. I want to share my happiness with you."

"It's kind of hard for me to be excited," she retorted. "How many marriages is this?"

I didn't answer.

"You are so your father's daughter."

My back and shoulders grew tense as trepidation turned into irritation.

"By the way, if you're interested, I had a baby girl, but you wouldn't know that since you always cut and run," she jabbed passive-aggressively, but I would not bite.

"Oh my god, Jul. That's amazing. Congratulations. What's her name?"

"Her name is Tess. She doesn't even know she has an aunt. In fact, Jack hardly remembers you at all. I am all alone, but hey, let's throw you a fucking party."

"Jesus, this is why I stay away. You are all so toxic. Stop bitching and moaning. Kick the asshole out and lock the doors if you are that unhappy. Time to grow up, Squirt, and take a stand."

She had wasted too many years trying to make an unhappy marriage work, and it wasn't. Sometimes the truth is ugly and hurts like hell.

"The way you do? Should I emulate you? Should I become a druggy? Should I fuck every man I come across and then claim to be a lesbian? Is that the magic formula for happiness?"

"Sometimes you can be downright evil, Julie. I assume that means you won't be coming to the wedding."

"While you are out gallivanting around the world, perpetually reinventing yourself, I am here, stuck in a quagmire of shit." Her voice echoed with righteous indignation. "I'm raising two children practically alone, trying to keep Mom from overdosing. Dad calls almost every day but hardly ever asks about my children or me. He only wants to know if you've contacted me. So do me a favor, call your fucking father."

"Fine. If you change your mind..." I gave her the date, time, and location of the wedding and begged her to keep it a secret.

"You're not inviting Mom and Dad... again?"

"No. They will ruin everything. Please don't tell Andrew either. I want to make this perfect. Julie, I need this, and I sincerely hope you'll come. I'm sorry I can't be the big sister you want me to be. I truly am, but I can't." My eyes stung with tears aching to be released. "I love you, Julie. I really do."

The quiet click on the other side occurred without fanfare.

It was a beautiful fall day in 2003. The leaves were at their peak, and the scent of autumn was in the air. I found my mind drifting to the past when Julie and I would collect leaves from the giant oak outside our house. We would spend hours hunting for the perfect ones. They couldn't have any rips or insect holes; we wanted them to be flawless. Once we had our treasure, we would pour some paint onto a paper plate, then carefully dip one side of the leaf. Next, we would press them onto pieces of notebook paper. We cut them out when they were dry and stuck them to our walls using scotch tape. They would remain plastered there until the next year, when we would do it all over again.

"Excuse me, Ms. Brennan, we need to get started. Would you mind showing us to the kitchen?" enquired the caterer in a pristine white chef's jacket.

"Of course. Please follow me," I led the way, snapping out of my trip down memory lane.

Within hours, they transformed our backyard into the most exquisitely charming wedding venue. White chairs sprinkled the grass on either side of a white satin runner, guiding everyone to their seats. A trellis with white roses weaving between the lattices marked the end of the aisle.

Maggie was getting ready in the guest room, and I dressed in ours.

"Time to get the show on the road," trumpeted Mayor Allen in his husky voice through the door. I glanced at the clock on the dresser; the numbers read 1:30, and I was ready to begin my life.

Maggie and I stepped out of our rooms at the exact same time. My heart quickened at the sight of her. She was more beautiful than I could have imagined. I thought, *this woman, this remarkable woman, will be mine. How on earth did I get so lucky?*

Maggie wore a short white dress with a sweetheart neckline and a simple pearl necklace that fell on her collarbone. Her legs were long and incredibly sexy in her pearled sling-backs, and her hair cascaded down her back in perfect chestnut and amber ringlets.

"You take my breath away." I was mesmerized by everything about her.

"You like?" Maggie twirled, giving me a full three-hundred-and-sixty-degree view.

"I love you in your oversized sweatpants and ratty old T-shirts, but wow, you are stunning."

I wore a long simple sheath of white satin with a plunging neckline and pearl drop earrings. My hair was in a low bun with a sprig of baby's breath woven around it.

"You don't clean up so badly yourself." Maggie winked.

"Don't forget your flowers," the wedding planner said, running into the hallway holding out two bouquets of calla lilies tied together with a white satin ribbon.

"Sarah, did you pick these out?"

I nodded my head in the affirmative, knowing they were her favorite.

"I love you so much," Maggie offered tenderly, and I believed her.

"Are you ready?" I beamed.

"I was born ready, baby. Let's do this."

We clasped hands as we walked out the door. All our new friends were in attendance to celebrate with us. Herman strummed an instrumental version of Little Guitars as we walked down the aisle.

The mayor cleared his voice and took the microphone to begin. "Ladies and Gentlemen, on behalf of Sarah and Maggie, I welcome you to this celebration of their love. Please, take your seats. Without further ado, I ask, who here gives these brides away?" My smile instantaneously faded. I forgot to tell him to take out that part, knowing no one would be here to do that job.

"I do," rang out a voice that has been with me throughout my life. "It would be my honor to give away my sister and her future wife."

Julie and my eyes locked, a knowing look passing between us. I held Maggie's hand tightly and nodded for the mayor to continue.

We are The Brennan Girls.

If you enjoyed this story, please consider leaving a review on Amazon or Goodreads. Authors love getting feedback from their readers.

https://linktr.ee/vikkialexander

Acknowledgments

Thank you, Tiffany Persaud, of Burden of Proofreading. You truly are my grammatical guru and quotation mark queen. All hail Queen Tiffany.

Thank you to all my beta readers: Jayne Lockwood, Sara Hovel, Donna Scuvotti, and Kristen Murray. I am incredibly grateful for your time, support, and feedback.

Thank you, Cindy Shelton, for yet again, being my first and most enthusiastic beta reader.

Thank you, Dr. Lisa Cappalletti, for spending hours dissecting the nuances of the human psyche with me.

Thank you, Daina Gonzalez, for being the keeper of all my secrets and making me laugh for over four decades.

Thank you, Louisa Corallo, for workshopping this with me during our hikes. Your support has been nothing short of amazing.

Thank you to MIBLArt for your patience and talent.

Thank you to Ray, Peter and Grace for cheering me on from the sidelines. You are all so very loved.

Last but not least, thank you to my Tenafly Chicks. You ladies fill my heart.

"There is no greater power in the Universe than the power of love." - The secret

Also By

Coloring Life

Looking at Julie, you would think she had it all. She's the type of woman who turns heads when she walks into a room. Her raven hair is always meticulously coiffed, with designer sunglasses perched upon her head. She has spent years crafting the perfect persona. However, living a privileged life is not all she thought it would be.

The man she once believed to be her prince charming shows his true colors. He takes control of every aspect of their lives, giving her nothing but heartache in return. The big house and fancy cars can't keep the demons of her childhood from invading her psyche. They remind her of the days when she was powerless.

Julie tries to resist her descent into depression with alcohol and sex, but some battles are too hard to fight. Maybe there is no such thing as a happily ever after for people like her, or maybe there is.

"This is a brilliantly observed slice of a parallel universe, hiding in plain sight," -Jane Lockwood, Lady Jane's Awesome Blog

"It felt like I was reading someone's diary. Each word revealing the thoughts closest to the heart of this woman." - Amazon

"Alexander writes with fluid honesty about the complexities of being a woman. -Raveaboutreading, Book Blogger

"Julie is such an amazingly complex woman that every married woman can relate to." -Amazon

"She holds a secret that threatens not only her own emotional stability but that of her marriage." Goodreads

Made in the USA
Middletown, DE
22 August 2022

71999627R00133